Hope Givers

Conversations and Stories of Hope

Jodi O'Donnell-Ames

Hope Givers

Copyright © 2023 by Jodi O'Donnell-Ames

All rights reserved.

No portion of this book may be reproduced in any form without written permission from the publisher or author, except as permitted by U.S. copyright law.

This publication is designed to provide accurate and authoritative information in regard to the subject matter covered. It is sold with the understanding that neither the author nor the publisher is engaged in rendering legal, investment, accounting or other professional services. While the publisher and author have used their best efforts in preparing this book, they make no representations or warranties with respect to the accuracy or completeness of the contents of this book and specifically disclaim any implied warranties of merchantability or fitness for a particular purpose. No warranty may be created or extended by sales representatives or written sales materials. The advice and strategies contained herein may not be suitable for your situation. You should consult with a professional when appropriate. Neither the publisher nor the author shall be liable for any loss of profit or any other commercial damages, including but not limited to special, incidental, consequential, personal, or other damages.

ISBN: 978-0-9990165-8-9

Grateful to Lauren Dougherty, Warren Benton Ames, Jack Tatar, Alina O'Donnell, and Allison Heller for their editing guidance. Cover design by Keiren Dunfee. Back cover design by Kai DeMarco. Back cover photo credit goes to Kapu Patel Photography.

To all of the HOPE GIVERS.

May you know them. May you be them.

For my brother Jamie- optimist and hope giver.

"Hope is being able to see that there is light despite all of the darkness." – Desmond Tutu

Contents

Praise for Hope Givers	VI
Foreword	1
Preface	4
1. Start Where You Are: Cultivating Your Life	10
2. Changing the Dialogue Through Emotional Intelligence and Forgiveness	28
3. Finders Keepers: Mentors Facilitate Change	36
4. Finding Resources: The Importance of Curiosity and Learning	46
5. Grinding the Grit Muscle and the Importance of Perseverance	54
6. Rule of Threes: Clarity of Purpose and Priorities	60
7. Finding your Fearless Five: The Power of Learning from Others	70
8. Dead Ant, Dead Ant: Integrating Power and Positivity Into Your Life	78
9. Good Will Hunting: Reframing Your Life After Loss	86
10. Anything and Everything: Behaviors, Habits, and Perseverance- Oh My!	96
11. Hope Personified	104
About the Author	110

Praise for Hope Givers

"Hope Givers is a powerful and inspirational culmination of stories, lessons, and resources for cultivating hope while overcoming adversity. Jodi and her many guests reflect on their most vulnerable experiences and share that hope, love, and company are the most essential tools needed to achieve resiliency and success."
*-Sammi B., **Certified Child Life Specialist***

"Jodi's book is an incredibly powerful tool in navigating the challenges that life often throws our way. Despite the hardships and pain, Jodi provides empathy, perspective and wisdom in recognizing and respecting this while seeking out and appreciating the ways in which hope can provide meaning and resilience in working through grief. Jodi has embodied the idea of turning pain into purpose, and I am inspired by her daily." *-**Betsy Piccolo, LPC***

"Written from the heart. This wonderful memoir relates the transformative value of learning from others when dealing with grief and the many other challenges that life throws in your way. Honest, compassionate, inspirational."
*-Fred Weber, **Founder of Weber Scientific, SCORE Mentor***

HOPE GIVERS

"*Hope Givers* will show you how to cope with challenging situations and gain hope. Most importantly, it will show you how to help others gain hope as well."
-Jack Tatar, Co-Author, "Cryptoassets: The Innovative Investors' Guide to Bitcoin & Beyond"

"Gracious, kind, thought-provoking, heartfelt, and comforting." *-Christopher MacLellan, M.A., Founder of The Whole Care Network*

"Hope Givers delves into the profound journeys of individuals navigating through immense diversity, yet it triumphs as a beacon of inspiration."
-Kristina Meyer, Developmental Interventionist and Special Education Teacher

Foreword

Among the greatest opportunities we experience is meeting someone new. Many of those who know me as the grumpy, opinionated New Yorker may find it surprising to hear that from me. Though I still proceed cautiously into interactions with new people, I also keep an open mind. There have been two people who have had the most impact on that "openness". One is my glorious wife of numerous decades, Maude, who when I met her in my teens made me say to myself, "I wanna be like her!" She saw the good in all people and challenged me to do so as well. Now into my seventh decade, I'm still chasing that dream. I've accepted that being half the person she is would be a major miracle.

The other person is the author of this book, Jodi O'Donnell-Ames. When I met Jodi over a decade ago, she told me her story. How ALS had taken her husband, and the caregiving travails that took place for her as a new mother and wife who knew that her husband would die. The Staten Island mentality I possessed had me questioning why she wasn't angrier and more distraught by her situation. The book you're holding will tell you Jodi's story. Why she has been able to not only cope with her situation, but also thrive and impact the lives of so many people with her story of hope. That story led to her creation of an organization called Hope Loves Company, which helps families face the realities of a fatal disease. Her efforts to help others transcend the ALS experience continues to provide hope to all those who need it, to deal with the troubles of their day-to-day existence. You have an inspiring tale ahead of you.

I'm fortunate to have two amazing children, Eric and Grace, in whom I've tried to instill the many lessons I've learned from not only my life, but also from those around me. One is that 'life is a marathon, not a sprint'. Often, life throws us curves. We notice others around us getting something or somewhere we'd like to have or be. It's not to judge what others have received, but rather serves to remind us that life is a long-term deal. Patience, gratitude, and hope are the key ingredients to getting what and where we want to be.

At some point, I believe that just about everyone finds themselves with their 'chin in the gutter'. Whether it's the loss of a loved one, or a job, or a home, or whatever we once possessed and now recognize as being gone from our lives, the emotions that place us at our "lowest point" can feel overwhelming with no escape or solution in front of us. People can tell us that we need to have hope; but what is it? How do we find hope when we are so far buried in our pain and anger? We need to move on, but how? How do we find hope in the face of such pain?

It's said that God doesn't give us more than we can handle. For those at these low points in their lives, this is a belief easily dismissed. Only with time, placing one foot in front of the other in the "marathon" of our life, will we be able to see the wisdom in it. When you meet the people in this book, you'll learn to appreciate the reality that everyone has their own stories to tell; their own wisdom from how they've addressed the times in their lives that felt hopeless.

You're not alone in these experiences.

This book will show you how to cope with these situations and gain hope. Most importantly, this book will show you how to help others gain hope as well. When you've found yourself in the gutter, maybe you were able to pick yourself up on your own. But, more than likely, you had someone reach out a helping hand to lift you up. It was that giving hope that may have ultimately made all the difference. May you read this book and not only find hope for yourself, but also discover how you can give hope to others—whether they are a loved one or someone you barely know. We all have our own stories, our own tragedies, and our own challenges. That said, we're all in this race together. May this book provide the solutions you need to keep you moving forward even in times of the toughest trials we face. –Jack Tatar, Author, "Cryptoassets: The Innovative Investors' Guide to Bitcoin & Beyond"

Jack Tatar is an author of numerous books including a book called 'Safe 4 Retirement: The Four Keys to a Safe Retirement' which he wrote after the deaths of his parents, and the best-selling "Cryptoassets: The innovative Investor's Guide to Bitcoin and Beyond". His publishing business, People Tested Media published Jodi's book "Someone I Love Has ALS", which is distributed to families dealing with an ALS diagnosis of a loved one. He was an early board member of Hope Loves Company and a driving force behind the creation of the Susan Anderson Scholarship, which provides college funding for a child from a family facing ALS.

Preface

Thank you for making the decision to buy my book. I appreciate that you're here to implement the following ideas in a way that supports your understanding, progress, and success. I think it's important to remind you that success looks different for everyone. Before you delve into these pages, allow yourself to daydream. For many years, I had a preconceived image of success. If you have been on Instagram or TikTok lately, you see images of success everywhere. The house, the cars, the clothes.

Those things did not appeal to me and my definition of success. Instead, I have concentrated on what I needed to be happy, the necessities, and then what I desire for my ideal life experience. After reflection, my happiness depended on my health, relationships, adventures, and financial security. You should consider your definition of success and what that looks like to you. Don't worry about what it looks like to anyone else, just you.

Hope Givers was written with hope, and without judgment, for anyone who wants to grow from where they are to where they want to be. In each chapter there are shared stories, resources, questions, and tips to inspire and challenge you along the way.

There have been countless days in my life when I was not happy, healthy, or helpful. It took decades to get to this place of healing and joy and I want the same thing for you.

Writing has always been cathartic for me so from the time I was ten years old, I was putting my thoughts to paper. I started with poems, essays and articles. In middle school, I joined the Sojourner Yearbook Committee, having no idea what sojourner meant. In Hebrew, a sojourner is a person or group residing either temporarily or permanently in a community that is not primarily their own, and is dependent on the "good-will" of that surrounding community for their continued existence.[1] The word meant little to me at 14, but now at 57, it has become self-evident. We are all sojourners in the human experience, only visiting for some time. Time is the only resource we can never replenish. Understanding this truth is an important step in bringing dreams to fruition. The time to begin is now.

So why am I putting my most vulnerable experiences into print? For the 16 million young adults who have not yet found a mentor.[2] For the baby boomers who are ready for something new. For those of us who've had the privilege of retiring, but are curious about what's next. It's for those who dream about being the very first family member to go to college, and are both scared and excited. I know that feeling, so I'm writing about what I know. Whether this is your first read about personal development or your fiftieth, I am proud of your commitment to bringing positive change into your life and I hope that you are too.

I didn't plan on writing a book, a podcast wrote it for me. In 2019, toward the beginning of the Covid-19 pandemic, I started my podcast, *Gratitude to Latitude, Stories of Resilience and Hope*. Our biggest challenges can result in our deepest clarity and creation and like everyone else, I was anxious and sad about the state of our world. Too much time on my hands led to too many thoughts and once I dwell on my hard times, it's a domino effect. So, I tried something new and started a podcast. I had no idea where that would take me, but it was an affordable and fun process. It required a few things: a microphone, laptop, great questions and guests. I had all of those things and selfishly, I wanted and needed to interview my Hope Givers, the people who have made me a better person. The ones who inspire me to show up with a smile, determination, and grit. The ones who remind me to never give up. So, I asked them to be my guests on G2L and the rest is history.

When it felt like life was falling apart in the midst of a pandemic, we came together virtually for powerful discussions. Our computers connected us from miles apart. So did our struggles and triumphs, and that's what ignited our conversations. We talked about growing up, education, health, loss, and success. We put everything on the table with nothing to lose. Those heartfelt conversations complement my story of hope, and are woven into the pages you are about to unfold.

It was a privilege to host a podcast and interview so many incredible people. A persistent theme from our conversations was that success takes patience, hard work, and time. There is no direct route. Sometimes progress seems effortless, while taking two or three steps in one leap, other times you might be stationary, confused whether to go up or down. You may even find yourself standing at the bottom of the stairs, looking up and feeling defeated. Steps are all a part of the personal growth paradigm. Every chapter holds ideas and tips that are steps for you to take. Your journey to success will not be easy or smooth. It will be peppered with frustration, exhaustion, and moments of defeat. But, it's your journey and your life and you are the only person who can turn your dreams into reality.

Speaking of dreams, *Hope Givers* includes many of my favorite authors and quotes. These are not just random quotes embedded in my narrative. The quotes included here were mantras, repeated several times daily and exposed to frustration and sweat. I depended on them to fuel my progress when I hit a wall. I hung them on my computer and refrigerator. I placed them in my books and on my planner. *Hope Givers* celebrates people, quotes, and the stories that support their significance. It's about building your relationships, support, resources, and confidence. Life is a journey of hope. If others have found the path to a happy and successful life, I know you can too.

Why *Hope Givers*?

We all have times in our lives when we feel hopeless. If we are fortunate, Hope Givers come into our lives exactly when we need them. Even better is when they stay in our lives and we somehow, someway, come to reciprocate hope. My journey has been enriched by those people.

In my home office I have a sign that says, *"The Journey IS the destination,"* which is paraphrased from Ralph Waldo Emerson's words, *"It's the journey, not the destination, that matters."*[3] I bought it from a dollar store when I was first dipping my toes in entrepreneurial waters. The sign was on my desk as an anchor to my grandiose expectations of myself and my accomplishments. I was working long days like a hamster on a wheel until I began recognizing the attributes in others that I wanted for myself. The courage of Peter Hall. The fearless personality of Jack Tatar. The bold grit of Sara Cooper. The quiet heroism of my husband Benton and late sister-in-law Kim.

Hope is written throughout this book and on my heart. The Hope Givers before you are examples of the friends, colleagues, partners and mentors you need in your life too.

So, how should you read this book? I recommend you grab a pen, some highlighters, a cozy spot, a friend, a partner, and begin. Everything starts at the beginning so that's where I will start too. As you read, mark pages, take notes, and put the content into action. Read the questions and write down your answers. Read on and follow up. Implement the suggestions into your daily habits and watch what happens. If I introduce you to a new author or concept, Google them.

Keep a journal and write down questions, key points, and highlight what resonates with you. When you put in the work, you will see an enormous change in your progress.

It's my turn to pay it forward and to be a hope giver too. I smile more. I hold doors open. I buy coffee for strangers. I leave positive mantras on cars. I coach, I speak, I train, I care. I see myself everywhere. A woman walking with her head down. A man in church, crying. I know that pain. I know that journey. While the stories that are shared here provide blatant hope, simple and random acts of kindness can provide hope too. Hope can switch our mindsets from nothing is possible to anything is possible. A random act of kindness can be the motivating catalyst we need to feel empowered and hopeful. Random acts of kindness offer a form of inspiration and encouragement. Life is a labyrinth of joy, pain, loss, uncertainty and hope, not a direct route to joy. Sometimes, it feels like it's a dream come true. Other times, we are simply trying to get through one moment or one day at a time. The more we recognize and celebrate those moments that lift our hearts and move us to happy tears, the more hopeful we become.

We are all just doing our best. My Hope Givers also needed hope at different points in their lives. The process wasn't always magical, perfect, or clear to them. The one thing that kept them all going through tough times was hope for what might be. Maureen teaches self-defense to empower women like herself. Sean climbs mountains because he can, and certainly not because it's easy.

People believed in me and I believe in you. I thank all of my Hope Givers, those included here and the countless others throughout my life, for elevating my soul and my belief in myself. The journey will break you. It will mold you. It will fuel you, and in the process, you will grow and be ready for your next destination.

*CW: The material throughout these chapters includes discussions of difficult material, e.g., abuse, assault, and suicide, that may be difficult or disturbing for readers. Please be advised.

---

1. Oxford Bibliographies. *(n.d.). Sojourner. obo.*
   https://www.oxfordbibliographies.com/abstract/document/obo-9780195393361/obo-9780 195393361-0266.xml

2. *The Mentoring Effect: Young People's Perspectives on the Outcomes and ...* (n.d.).
   https://www.mentoring.org/wp-content/uploads/2019/12/The_Mentoring_Effect_Executi ve_Summary.pdf

3. Irey, Eugene F., and Ralph Waldo Emerson. "A Concordance to Five Essays of Ralph Waldo Emerson: Nature, the American Scholar, the Divinity School Address, Self-reliance, Fate." *Garland Pub. eBooks*, 1981, ci.nii.ac.jp/ncid/BA17248048.

Chapter One

Start Where You Are: Cultivating Your Life

"It doesn't matter where you are coming from. All that matters is where you are going." -Brian Tracy

My Hope Givers have made me who I am and my list of accomplishments would not exist without them. That list began when I was a child; it first included family, clergy, teachers, and coaches. It grew to include mentors, in-laws, and community leaders. Eventually, my dearest friends, spouses, children, and grandchildren have become my biggest hope givers. Words are inadequate in expressing my sincere gratitude, but they know that I love and appreciate them. They know that our relationships have built my foundation.

Those relationships have taught me about self-love, self-respect, self-empathy and self-care. They also reminded me to be gentle with myself, more patient when I fail, and less discouraged on hard days. There have been so many hard days.

It's interesting to me that by the time we are six or seven years old, we begin declaring who we will become. Dancers. Firefighters. Teachers. Professional football players. We start with big aspirations. That's why the journey, not the destination, is so important. We evolve in the process. We become who we are meant to be. While I always knew who I wanted to be, I just didn't have a process for getting there. What I did understand was that it would require enormous effort and resources. I knew it would require me to change my outlook, my habits, and expectations.

At the age of seventeen, choosing my school senior superlative reflected that knowledge.

It took courage to write a stanza, rather than something witty, under my picture. It took courage to be different. It took courage to realize that, like it or not, how I achieved my goals was completely up to me.

R.L. Sharp's poem, *A Bag of Tools* [1]

Each is given a bag of tools,

A shapeless mass,

A book of rules;

And each must make—

Ere life is flown—

A stumbling block

Or a stepping-stone.

Around that time of change and transition, I discovered something true. You can't build a healthy life without a strong foundation. If you were denied that opportunity, for whatever reason, you have the power to build your own. I recognized that some of my foundation was weak, and that was both overwhelming and frustrating. As an athlete, who played soccer, lifted weights, and had the school record for the girls' arm hang, I knew that I wanted to feel physically strong. But I also needed to get mentally strong too. I needed a powerful mindset.

According to renowned psychologist and author Carol Dweck, a mindset is "*a self-perception, or self-theory*" that individuals hold about themselves. Believing that you are either "intelligent or unintelligent" is a simple example of a mindset."[2]

Nearly a million copies of *Mindset: The New Psychology of Success* have been purchased. New phrases like 'fixed' and 'growth mindsets' are being integrated into schools, businesses, and professional athletics. Importantly, if we all had a growth mindset without skipping a beat, there would be no such market for the research nor self-help or self-improvement books that discuss it. So, an important question is, do you have a growth mindset? As Ms. Dweck explains in her book, "*in a growth mindset, you look for what you've learned. You don't know what your abilities are until you make a full commitment to developing them.*" Or, do you have a fixed mindset? She explains the difference: "*In a fixed mindset, people believe their basic qualities, like their intelligence or talent, are simply fixed traits.*" Put another way: Do you believe in your ability to change the story of who you are?

In my early twenties, as a teacher, I was struggling financially. I didn't make a lot of money teaching, I was paying off my student loans, my car, then there was the matter of my insurance, my rent, and by the end, I was barely able to pay for groceries. I was trying to build a strong foundation that needed patching. I dwelled on the fact that there were people who started out ahead of the game. They didn't owe for their college educations, they didn't buy their first car and hell, they also wouldn't be paying for their wedding one day, and might even get a generous gift towards their first house. I was jealous. *If only that were my life.* Starting out your young adulthood with those privileges makes it so much easier. If I didn't start out in debt, my foundation would have been stronger, right? I fixated on what I didn't have until I came to the realization that my thoughts weren't going to change anything. Jealousy wouldn't change anything. In fact, feeling that way made me feel badly about myself which only fueled the negativity. I was embarrassed that I even entertained those thoughts.

That's when I knew that my outlook needed a makeover.

For the first two decades of our lives, as children, students, and young adults, the conditions of our positive mindsets depend mostly on the people around us. The brain takes a long time to develop and research has found that while it may not grow in size after the teen years, it will still continue to develop well into the twenties.[3] No matter your age, if you have come to terms with the fact that you don't have a positive mindset, or a growth mindset, that's ok. From now on, you are in charge of your thoughts and your progress. No one else can do that for you. They also don't have the ability to make you feel less than. It's just as Eleanor Roosevelt described: "No one can make you feel inferior without your consent."

As a young adult, with little money, I felt inferior and that was my own doing. It's important to have concrete goals and dreams that are empowered by self-awareness and emotional intelligence, before taking on huge objectives. It's important to harness your skills and accept your challenges. I became a coach in my fifties because I needed one. I needed accountability. I needed encouragement. I needed someone to look at my goals and to break them into actionable steps. My personal journey gave me my coaching tagline: "Mindset is the launchpad to all things possible. Wellness fuels the process."[4] Having the right mindset is important, and your mind lives in your body, so taking care of your body is just as important. In a nutshell, you need both to get optimal results and that's why the phrase works. That's why we'll touch on all of these concepts throughout this book. Without first understanding who we are, and why we want and do the things we do, we cannot fully understand how to move forward. That's why historians study the past to best understand the future.

You may have heard of American professor, lecturer, author, and podcast host, Brené Brown. If not, Brené is an expert in many things, but mostly on these timely topics: shame, courage, empathy, and vulnerability. Brené's twenty years of emotion research show us that, "*Hope is not an emotion, it's a way of thinking or a cognitive process.*" She also notes that hope is 100% teachable, as well as the relevance of this teaching through being raised by hopeful parents. Her insight and perspective only further emphasize my understanding of the role that hope plays in our lives.[5]

Hope is about rescuing what we thought was lost. It's about creating a better future. When we marry the right mindset with the right tools and resources, possibilities become tangible. As a matter of fact, it's your personal responsibility to build the life you have imagined for yourself. It's actually your right, and no one can deprive you of that right but yourself. You have the power and the choice to orchestrate the life and success you imagine. So get started.

Mark the pages that most resonate with you. My favorite books look like they are loved. Their pages have ears and words are circled and highlighted. Their covers are soft and torn. They sit by my bed and rarely get returned to the shelf where they belong.

Post these quotes on your computer, notebook, and on your desk. Seek inspiration and knowledge and believe in yourself. This can be the start to many wonderful things and you should be proud of your determination.

My journey began in the sixties.

I grew up in a small, 2.6 square mile town in South Jersey. We were blue collar workers. We were gritty, not educated. We were just across from Philadelphia, Pennsylvania, and die-hard Eagles fans. My mother Catherine was a hostess and my late father Peter (Peck) was a paver.

While neither had a formal education, they were both smart and hardworking and knew how to make ends meet. Well into mid-life, when speaking at huge venues or sipping coffee at a local chamber, I tried to circumvent sharing my humble beginnings. When you surround yourself with highly educated people and mentors, as I do and recommend, it's sometimes difficult to share the truth. I remember when my teen daughter Alina, who was raised in an affluent town, with college expectations and socioeconomic privileges, asked about my college legacy. My response was, "I went to college and that's my legacy!"

Today I embrace and share every success gained against all odds. I share my failures too.

I am authentic and it feels good to be honest.

In order to reach success, we need to be honest. At one point I remember taking a good look in the mirror and asking myself: Who are you? What are your strengths, your challenges, your beliefs and ideals? These questions build our self-awareness. Self awareness is defined as "conscious knowledge of one's own character, feelings, motives, and desires." The term was first introduced in 1972 by Shelley Duval and Robert Wicklund.[6] Bringing awareness to my thoughts, feelings and objectives increased my chances for success. Psychology 101. I wish I'd known more about the concept of self-awareness as a young adult, professionally as a teacher, personally in my relationships, and as a learning parent.

Though I didn't know the term, I had a form of intuitive understanding. From the time that I was a young adult, I thought about the life I was creating, and the legacy I'd leave behind. I was aware of my strengths and my challenges, and to this day, I don't refer to my challenges as weaknesses. I don't recommend you do either. There have been several events in my life that have left me empty, depressed, and unable to see a way out of hopelessness. But, I was never weak. I was a strong, young woman facing challenges. As much as we may wish for perfect lives, the truth is that life is messy and far from perfect. All of our experiences create our stories, and those stories matter. While I had a grip on who I was and what I wanted, I simply didn't have the tools to change what I didn't like. Coping tools were not a part of my upbringing. Chaos felt normal. How do you create a new normal when you don't know what normal is?

It sometimes felt like a whirlwind at home. We lived paycheck to paycheck and didn't have the means for extravagance. When I was fourteen, I bought a new bike with my paper route and confirmation money. It was a $100 Huffy ten speed.

My dad looked at it, smiled, and shared that all of his bikes, his clothes, and his shoes were hand-me-downs. My dad didn't say much, but when he did, I listened. It was a tough life for my parents. It made me sad that they fought. It made me sad that they got married so young and struggled financially. It made me sad that they had to leave school as children because of the Depression, buried under the weight of their responsibilities at home to make ends meet. That sadness weighed heavily on me. I recognized the generations of similar struggles and I appreciate, with great respect, all that my parents did for the five of us. Their lives were hard and they were products of their circumstances. Many of us have witnessed generations of families who struggle because of the same circumstances, the same behaviors, the same decisions, culminating in the same results. That's where I committed to a promise.

I chose to end that cycle and be the change I wished to see. Changing the dialogue doesn't mean that I am not grateful. I am grateful for everything my upbringing taught me about expectations. I learned how to be respectful, disciplined, kind, caring, and hard working. Those things have served me well in life and in work. Ultimately, changing the dialogue meant: expanding my self-awareness, making informed decisions, valuing my choices and their outcomes and having a greater understanding of both who I was and who I wanted to be. Self-awareness means recognizing that I am prone to depression and that it's ok to ask for help. It means not being embarrassed by crying easily or carrying pain.

In my late twenties, while caring for my terminally ill husband Kevin two years into our marriage, my hopelessness and depression collided in a zenith of despair. Before our world of ALS, or Lou Gehrig's disease, Kevin and I had an idyllic marriage, a two-year-old daughter, and the world at our fingertips. The news of a terminal illness changed all our plans. It changed everything but our love for one another and our daughter. As we battled life with ALS, our families and friends were very caring and present, but none of them were in this situation. No one else was dressing and bathing their thirty-four-year-old husband. No one else was planning their husband's funeral. No one else was preparing their husband's eulogy. It was surreal, scary, and traumatic. I felt alone and that is no one's fault, it just is. The person who I needed to console me could not hold me, speak, or tell me things would be ok. He could not wipe my tears, even though he desperately wanted to. He could listen and he did. He showed his love for me with his smile and his eyes. While intellectually I knew I had to accept what was happening, I wanted to have a screaming and kicking tantrum and demand, "Why is this happening?"

No matter what, we will all go through times that leave us asking, "Why?" It's inevitable. I wanted to hear, "Everything will be ok." But, that would have been a lie. While I understood things happen that are out of our control, I desperately wanted to have control. I wanted a miracle- our personalized, prayers answered, alleluia miracle.

As a caregiver for many years, I faced additional battles. The caregiving world is a quiet world. It's a massive, yet unseen world. Rosyln Carter summed it up beautifully, "There are four kinds of people in the world. There are those who were caregivers, those who are caregivers, those who will be caregivers, and those who will need caregivers."[7] That's a hard pill to swallow. Most of us don't want to think about sickness, caregiving, or loss until we have to. We focus on living, not dying.

When my late husband Kevin was losing his battle daily, I got into a really dark place. I tried to go to caregiver support groups, but that didn't work. I sat listening. "My wife's osteoporosis means she can't help me with the yardwork." And, "I don't want to care for my husband any longer." I left feeling worse. If I wasn't being a mom or a caregiver, I was lost. I didn't feel like getting out of bed. Showering was a chore. I canceled plans to meet with friends. I was a lump of grief fueled by coffee for survival. I lost weight, faith and my personality. I just wanted to shut the curtains and shut down. I wanted to disappear.

My grief began when Kevin was diagnosed with ALS in May of 1995 at University of Pennsylvania Hospital. It was Memorial Day weekend and we were supposed to be on the beach. Building sandcastles. Eating ice-cream. Diggin our toes into the sand.

But we were stuck in a horror movie.

Grief is a bully.

It robbed me of sleep.

It robbed me of hunger.

It interrupted my thoughts. It made me cry.

It rendered me into a fetal position.

It robbed me of hope.

I had no idea that grief would continue to play a role in my life for many years to come. What happened to the happy, creative, fun, adventurous person I was? I wouldn't see all of her again for nearly a decade. Once again, Hope Givers came into my life. It is said that there are no coincidences. No matter what I am facing, I believe there is a guiding presence in my life. For me personally, I believe that's God. My friend Neil reminds me to focus on my faith and Psalm 46:10 (King James Version), "Be still, and know that I am God." Whatever you may or may not believe, I hope that you feel supported spiritually as well. We all need something bigger than us to believe in. We all need to feel unconditional love.

Luckily, I didn't stay in the fetal position for long. I knew I had to stand up and face the music. Under the blanket of grief and fear, the shell of who I was remained. I wanted and needed to move forward. Slowly, in moments of rest and clarity, I started to recover. I was a leader who wanted to make a positive impact on the world. I was broken then healed, then broken again. I was a mom and caregiver who sometimes battled profound sadness. I was a wife and advocate too. With every setback, there was a friend willing to lend a hand. One of those people was Peter Hall, and he initiated my understanding of grief and healing.

Pete's daughter Alaina and my daughter Alina were classmates. We met at a school function, and something or someone connected us right there and then, in the middle of a field of running, screaming six-year-olds. You never know what is promised for us in life, or when glimpses of hope might find us. Pete was the first guest on my podcast because he was the original hope in my healing. We are both old souls. We are both aware of how far we've come, and how far we have to go. To this day, I can't exactly explain why, but it was like seeing a best friend for the first time in years. Maybe it was his understanding of grief too.

Before I continue, here's what I want you to know about my friend Pete. He is living proof of a strong mindset and incredible grit. He is also patient and caring: a combination that is hard to find. Pete is also a hope giver.

At the age of five, roaming through a field by himself, he dreamed of flying an airplane and his young vision was clear. He wanted to be a United States Air Force pilot, yet none of his family members had careers in aviation. As a pilot in the U.S. Air Force, Pete was deployed to Iraq and Afghanistan fifteen times between 1991 to 2004, with over two hundred missions of combat. It's hard to imagine my friend there, in the midst of a war.

Five-year-old Pete probably never expected to fly more than fifteen types of planes, four different military jets, at least ten different models of airliners, and countless General Aviation airplanes to numerous countries and destinations. Pete has seen and lived through some serious trauma. Five-year-old Pete also never expected to almost burn to death. Or to lose a son to suicide. Five-year-old Pete was full of hope, not loss. During our podcast interview, as I looked at Pete all these years later, I was proud of our coping and healing, of our letting go of the things we could no longer try to understand or control.

Pete knows who he is and lives an authentic life. "*We really can't be our authentic selves and show up for others if we're not being honest with who we are and what we're capable of. I think of it as if you want a good teammate, you have to be a good teammate. Part of that commitment is to say, I am limited right now. To know you have a limitation, even if you can't pinpoint what it is–to say my feelings have control of me right now–is enough to communicate as a teammate. To say, "Okay, maybe he's operating at a degraded level, and I understand what that's like," instead of going, "What the hell is wrong with you?"*

In 2005, Pete lost his oldest child, Aaron, age sixteen, to suicide. I still remember when Aaron was kind enough to play chess with my Kevin. At the time, Kevin was having difficulty moving the pieces, and Aaron waited patiently while we communicated each move and acted accordingly. Though only fourteen, Aaron demonstrated a compassion and patience beyond most adults. Most teen boys were playing video games, thinking about dating, dreaming about cars or their first beer. Aaron, as sweet as he was, was spending his free time bringing joy to a dying man. There was Aaron, with indecisive Kevin and chess ignorant me, patiently waiting for our next poorly orchestrated move.

We all know that no good news comes at 3 am. I remember the call, the tears and the voice that shared the news of Aaron's death in the middle of the night. My heart sank with grief, with memories and with the thought of never seeing Aaron again. In 2009, I received another early morning call. Pete had suffered a freak boating accident that left him with burns over sixty percent of his body. I was told that he was in stable condition and to pray for him.

It took Pete sixteen months of therapy to be able to return to work. Today, he still lives with constant pain as the result of burns, scarring and nerve damage. If you are reading this, you might be thinking, "How can one person be subjected to so much loss?" You may also be wondering, "What is Pete like today?"

I stay in touch with Pete and can tell you that he is not angry, mean, or disgruntled. Nor is he hopeless, defeated, or in despair. Pete, on the contrary, is the definition of a survivor. In the Cambridge dictionary, a survivor is a person *who continues to live, despite almost dying and a person who is able to continue living his or her life successfully despite experiencing difficulties.*[8] When you meet Pete, you feel comforted. He is peaceful and loving. Unless you get to know him personally, you have no idea of the hell he's endured. He doesn't carry it with him. He does not wear it as armor. He not only has risen from the unimaginable, but he has helped others do the same:

> "When I engage with someone, I listen. Listen to what others share both verbally and non-verbally. How do you feel when you know that someone just heard what you said? It's a gift to turn off the noise and deeply listen to others who need you."

Listening is something I always need to be cognizant of, and it's something we all could improve. Pete has recognized there's something healing about helping others. I agree. He uses his experiences to impact lives for the better. For him, it's less about where he's coming from, and far more about where he is going:

> "Listening creates a foundation that exists even when you are not there in person. I think, "Who out there can help this person?" It's part humility and part wisdom. I might not be the person who can help, but maybe I know someone who can."

There is so much we can learn from this one journey of hope. Pete has consistently chosen it over fear. He continues to create visions for his future, as well as the steps and the process of making those visions reality. Pete has challenged his mindset and rallied his discipline to stick to his goals, especially through difficult times. No matter what has happened, he believes that life is an exciting adventure. Because he treats life with that attitude, it feels that way.

Today, Pete looks forward to a very successful future with a flight or two in a plane he's currently building himself, a CubCrafters Carbon Cub EX-3. I'd say that Pete has earned his wings in more ways than one. Sadly, I know several families who have lost a loved one to suicide. That's also why I want you to know about 988. Dialing this hotline will put you or someone you love in touch with help immediately. If we are lucky, we get to live a long-life learning who we are and what gives us purpose, both despite and because of the pain or hopelessness we encounter. So, how do we even begin that process when so many challenges interrupt our dreams? How do we carry on?

A long time ago, while having coffee in town, a girlfriend shared a powerful tool with me, and I believe that both Pete and I have implemented this tool into our lives. It's common for us to more readily reserve forgiveness, compassion, patience, acceptance, and understanding for others. It's a lot harder to give ourselves the same grace. After a sip of coffee, my friend took a piece of my cookie and said, *"Do you remember how I called you in a panic last week and you told me to be gentle with myself?"*

"Of course," I replied.

"So why do you only reserve that support for others and not yourself?" she asked.

Self-love can be a challenge for all of us. It certainly has been for me. Growing up, we didn't talk about coping methods, mindful meditation, or getting proper rest. It wasn't in our repertoire. But with each birthday celebration, I respect myself and my journey more. I am just now making time for self-care. My experiences remind me that we need to give ourselves the same reverence we give to others. It's important to allow ourselves patience, healing, and a chance for hope. We always have the power to write our stories, even the rewrites.

Recently, I have been reading more about trauma and its effect on self-esteem.[9] I'm only scratching the surface of how it has molded my fears. My daughter Alina will remind me of things that we did while her dad was sick and I have no recollection of that time. My mother can't believe how much I can't remember when her ninety-year-old brain recalls everything. At one point, when Kevin needed medication, I was standing in the middle of a grocery store and I had no idea how I had gotten there. I was so sleep deprived, but we needed food and prescriptions. So there I was, like a deer in headlights in the middle of the cereal aisle, having a panic attack at 1 am. Learning about trauma helps me to better understand myself and my behaviors, so I am a dedicated student.

World-renowned trauma researcher Dr. Gabor Mate describes trauma as *"a psychic wound that hardens you psychologically that then interferes with your ability to grow and develop. It pains you and now you're acting out of pain. It induces fear and now you're acting out of fear. Trauma is not what happens to you, it's what happens inside you as a result of what happened to you."*[10]

He further explains in his book, *In the Realm of Hungry Ghosts*, that *"the greatest damage done by neglect, trauma or emotional loss is not the immediate pain they inflict but the long-term distortions they induce in the way a developing child will continue to interpret the world and her situation in it."* His words render me speechless.

If you have a therapist or mental health practitioner, you may have heard of the A.C.E. Score.[11] If you haven't learned about it and it's uncharted territory, I advise that you learn with the support of a professional. This information may be a trigger and I don't want you to address the concepts alone. I didn't learn about the A.C.E Score until I was well into my forties. I received a one-page resource sheet about the A.C.E. score at a children's conference and a bell went off. How did this term not cross my path? A.C.E. stands for Adverse Childhood Experiences, and the score is a tally of different types of abuse, neglect, and other adverse childhood experiences. A higher score indicates a higher risk for health problems later in life. I have personally checked yes to many of the A.C.E questions.

Along with our minds, our bodies keep score of trauma. On a cloudless afternoon in May, 1979, I witnessed tragedy. My friends, Billy and Tim, were playing soccer at our middle school field, along with hundreds of children and coaches. A few hundred yards away, my friend Deb and I were spying on our crushes. Ironically, we were giggling when it happened. A loud boom and a flash of light knocked us and everyone on the crowded school field to their knees.

Everyone slowly got up, in a daze, uncertain of what had just happened. I wiped off my dirty knees and said, "*What the hell was that?*" As Deb and I got acclimated, we looked over at Billy and Tim. They were motionless. A powerful lightning bolt had hit Billy directly at the goal post. Tim was saved by the soccer ball at his feet. Billy, age fourteen, died on the way to the hospital.

You can't witness something so horrific and shocking and continue life as it was. My childhood ended on May 23, 1979 at the age of thirteen. My initiation into adulthood was the senselessness that life could propose, prevailed in my thoughts and actions. I was crestfallen. I know that this was among the moments that changed me; I no longer believed in anything.

Nothing was as it seemed. Friends and life could be here one moment and gone the next. It took me two years to navigate that trauma. To give it a name. To learn how to verbalize my feelings and for the nightmares to subside.

I began this chapter with Brian Tracy's quote because it empowers me. But, I think one thing does matter regarding where you are coming from: Perspective. The behaviors, habits, and characteristics that got you to this moment in time, may be different than the ones that bring you forward. I know mine are for sure. Your perspective, like your behaviors and habits, is meant to change and grow with you. You are a tangible evolution of the human spirit.

Questions to consider:

Are you aware of your feelings, goals, strengths and challenges?

Are you struggling emotionally?

Is trauma holding you back?

Do you practice healthy coping skills such as yoga, deep breathing or meditation?

Noteworthy:

Keep an emotional journal to write down your feelings.

Take a self-awareness test to better understand where you are in the process.[12]

Find a support group near you to help you process your feelings.

---

1. Poems For Kids. "A Bag of Tools R.L. Sharpe-Rainy Day Poems." *Rainy Day Poems*, 18 Mar. 2022, http://rainydaypoems.com/poems-for-kids/inspirational-poems/a-bag-of-tools-r-l-sharpe.
2. Dweck, Carol S. *Mindset: The New Psychology of Success*. Ballantine Books, 2007.
3. *Understanding the Teen Brain – Health Encyclopedia-University of Rochester Medical Center*.
   http://www.urmc.rochester.edu/encyclopedia/content.aspx?ContentTypeID=1&ContentID=305

4. "Jodi O'Donnell-Ames." *JoaSpeaksOn*, Sept. 2020, http://www.joaspeakson.com/about.

5. Brown, Brené. *The Gifts of Imperfection: Let Go of Who You Think You're Supposed to Be and Embrace Who You Are*. Simon and Schuster, 2010.

6. Miller, Kori D. "Using Self-Awareness Theory and Skills in Psychology."

7. Snelling, Sherri. "Rosalynn Carter: A Pioneering Caregiving Advocate Says More Must Be Done." *Next Avenue*, 6 Aug. 2012, http://www.nextavenue.org/rosalynn-carter-pioneering-caregiving-advocate-says-more-must-be -done/#.

8. *Survivor*. 3 May 2023, http://dictionary.cambridge.org/us/dictionary/english/survivor#.

9. "Trauma and Low Self Esteem - Khiron Clinics." *Khiron Clinics*, 14 June 2019, http://khironclinics.com/blog/trauma-and-low-self-esteem/#:~:text=According%20to%20the%20study%2C%20E2%80%9Cthe,decline%20in%20self%2Desteem%E2%80%9D.

10. Maté, Gabor. *In The Realm of Hungry Ghosts: Close Encounters With Addiction*.

11. "Take the ACE Quiz – and Learn What It Does and Doesn't Mean - Center on the Developing Child at Harvard University." *Center on the Developing Child at Harvard University*, 30 May 2019, http://developingchild.harvard.edu/media-coverage/take-the-ace-quiz-and-learn-what-it-does-and-doesnt-mean.

12. Staff, iNLP Center, and iNLP Center Staff. "Self Awareness Test – Discover Your Hidden Opportunity for Growth and Success." *iNLP Center*, Sept. 2021, http://inlpcenter.org/self-awareness-test.

Chapter Two

Changing the Dialogue Through Emotional Intelligence and Forgiveness

"I am not a product of my circumstances, I am a product of my decisions." -Steven Covey

We all have our stories, and they begin with childhood. I have never met an adult who said their parents did a perfect job. I know I haven't been a perfect parent, and being one is not an easy role for imperfect humans to have. It's a huge responsibility to raise happy and healthy children. If parenting were an official job, we probably wouldn't get hired, based on the extended criteria and expectations of the position. Are you willing to be sleep deprived for days, months, and likely years in this role? Are you willing to work endless hours, overtime on weekends, and without pay for this team? Unlike most important things, being a parent does not require instructions, a license or a certificate of mastery. One minute we are thinking about having children, and the next we are trying to explain why you must look both ways before crossing the street to a distracted preschooler who needs a bathroom now.

My parents worked constantly. They were concentrating on paying the bills, and keeping us fed, safe, and clean, all of which was nearly impossible. We had huge appetites, something was always breaking in our century-old house, and we were heavily involved in sports which meant dirty knees and cleats. Plus, no one knew where we were (or how to find us) when we had scooters, bikes, and cars to travel independently with no cell phones or GPS tracking devices. My parents demanded a lot from us. They had big expectations about core values: manners, attitudes, and determination. My mother nurtured the young children next door when they lost their mom to cancer. She hugged them, bought them gifts, and welcomed them into our home day and night. I learned my generosity, servitude, and caregiving from her.

My father worked several jobs to provide for us and even then, money was tight. He paved many of the first streets and parking lots in South Jersey, most of the time in the hot summer sun on the hot summer asphalt. My mother was a hostess, she made flower arrangements and later, she drove a school bus and even opened a deli. They did everything they could to provide for us, but there were things that I felt were missing.

Writer's listen. We observe. We take mental notes. All of my experiences are imprinted in my mind, reverently taking space. By the time I was twelve, I knew that getting some form of education was key to my progress. I knew that being in control of my emotions and knowing how to self-regulate was important too. That was a big one but again, I came late to the game. I also knew that I needed to hold space for forgiveness to evolve. Some part of me knew these skills were connected.

Although I look back for perspective, I don't stay there. Staying there would entice blame, and blame does not serve me or anyone well. I now understand that staying there would impede my ability to move forward, but that wasn't always the case. For years, I was a competitive player in the blame game. I was a great defense player. I pointed fingers and dodged introspection and solutions. The term *emotional intelligence* is defined as *"the ability to identify and handle one's emotions along with the emotions of others."* **(16)** This discovery was life changing for me. Practicing emotional intelligence is a personal and daily commitment, especially when I am stressed.

When I struggled as a freshman in college, I blamed my poor grades on my upbringing and the fact that my parents did not prioritize any form of education and weren't involved in mine. We've all been there. It's easier to blame others than to admit our perspective is flawed. It's even easier to play the blame game when you are struggling and someone else is succeeding. I wanted to be able to enjoy college without the huge financial worry that weighed on my shoulders. Gas. Food. Classes. Books. Notebooks. It was easier to skip meals and get money back at the end of the semester than to work a fourth job.

Every day we are inundated with questions that help us to make decisions. Some of those questions are routine and require little thought. What will I wear today? What will I have for breakfast? Which route will I take to work? Other questions require deeper thought and planning. What do I want to be when you grow up? Will I go to college or learn a trade? Will I get married? Will I have children? Why did this happen? Will I be able to forgive?

Forgiving is the opposite of blaming. It's about letting go of resentment toward someone who has committed a wrong against you. It's the choice to make a conscious decision: To let go of our anger and all of the feelings wrapped around the injustice we cannot control. Forgiving is hard because it means we release our grip on the story as we've been telling it. It could mean letting go of hurt, anger, pride, or expectations. It could mean all of the above and more.

Somehow, my friend Maureen Pierce chose forgiveness. Her story is a reminder that we can begin to heal even the most adverse childhood experiences by learning to move forward with them.

In 1976, in Kenosha Wisconsin, Maureen, her mother, and her friend Heidi, were playing at a local park, having fun. This day, Maureen wanted to do something sweet for her mom, running off to pick some wild flowers. The flowers were in the park, but just down the hill from where they were standing. Unfortunately, there was a man hiding and waiting at the bottom of the hill for his next victim. Eight-year-old Maureen was abducted from the park in broad daylight. In the middle of nowhere and in the hands of her assaulter, Maureen knew that her only hope was to run for her life. So, when her attacker stepped away for a moment, that is exactly what she did.

While we can't erase the feelings of being abused or hurt, we can choose how we want to move forward. That's where our power lives. In meeting Maureen, you know immediately she's beautiful, kind, and polite. What most people don't see at first glance is that Maureen is a power house of resilience. She's an expert in RAD (Rape Agression Defense) and could bring you to your knees in seconds if necessary. **(17)** For many years, however, Maureen tried to suppress what happened to her–as though she was responsible for it.

"I blamed myself. I felt a lot of shame and guilt over the years. I felt like it was my fault.

So, I tried to shove it down, slap a smile on my face, and be strong."

It took her decades to begin taking her power back. In college, Maureen signed up for a martial arts class. She became a certified Rad Kids instructor in 2012, and then a certified RAD Woman in 2015. Her training was the first step in reclaiming her voice, her power, and her hope.

"The intense training helped me face some deep-seated fears and emotions. That is when I started talking about "my story" more openly. But healing is a lifelong

journey, I think. I believe we must face the trauma and process it. I spent so many years pushing it down, and we know that doesn't work! We can always grow. We can always learn new things."

There are times when I see a young child and think about Maureen at that age. I think about her choices to forgive her assaulter, to sign up for that first self-defense class. I think about her choice to share her story so that others may learn from or feel comforted by her experience. I think about both her vulnerability and her courage, and I am grateful to call her friend and mentor. Maureen wants every woman and child to have the power and confidence to protect themselves. She's committed to her mission.

"What I have learned through becoming a RAD (Rape Agression Defense), instructor is that trusting our gut–our intuition–and getting some sort of training, so that you can quickly act and don't freeze, is incredibly important." Maureen also realized that once she started teaching self-defense, she was far from healed. *"I was teaching a class, but hadn't really healed myself. A lot of people avoid that because they don't want those really deep, hurtful things brought up. But without going through that, and without bringing that up, you really can't heal what you don't acknowledge."*

We all deserve to feel safe in the world and along our journey. Like many victims of assault and rape, Maureen wrestled for years with guilt, anxiety, stress, fear, and shame. She also thought that if she didn't talk about what had happened, as well-meaning family and friends suggested, her trauma would eventually become a faded memory. That never happened and this pattern is familiar. As we now understand, trauma changes the brain. Unless you are aware of that fact, you don't have the tools to address it. Trauma means *extensive loss and grief*.[1] Pretending like something never happened doesn't work for anyone. When terrible things happen, we need to process them. That begins with verbalizing what happened. Once Maureen began to speak about her trauma, she also began to feel empowered. So much of our lives is not about our plans, hopes, nor dreams. So much is about the life-changing events that we never expected nor wanted—the things that interrupt those plans, hopes and dreams—and the journey we take to find our way back. We are all, in some way, constantly trying to find our way back from a fall.

Forgiveness is tricky when it involves a friend or family member, but it's even harder when it involves something that's happened to you directly. If you hold anger toward someone, you can't help but hold anger in your body. It's nearly impossible to separate the negative emotions towards someone without feeling the consequences of it yourself. Anger can boil into resentment and it can rob us of gratitude. When we choose to forgive those who we feel have wronged us, we free them from what has happened. Even more importantly, we also free ourselves.

I have a practice for letting go of anger. If it's face to face, I take a deep breath and wait ten seconds before responding. This simple practice has saved me from several otherwise dramatic scenes and thus, eventual apologies. If someone has angered you from afar, grab a piece of paper and put your emotions into writing. Despite all of the pain, abuse, and anger, Maureen chose forgiveness. Her decision, I believe, freed her of enormous resentment. When I talked to Maureen, I was reminded about my choices. Do I hold grudges? Do I blame others for my shortcomings? Am I still living the blame game? In order to grow, we need to ask ourselves the tough questions. If we don't like the answers, we're in control. Maureen could have easily taken a different route. She could have been a victim for the rest of her life, but she chose to be a fighter and today, continues to teach women how to be fighters too.

Questions to consider:

Are the terms self-awareness and emotional intelligence a part of your journey? Are there grudges you feel yourself holding onto?

Do these feelings serve your progress in any way?

Can you acknowledge those feelings, understand that they are normal (we are human and we make mistakes), and refocus your thinking towards self-compassion?

Are there feelings that you would benefit from sharing and processing with a counselor or therapist?

Noteworthy:

Find out your Emotional Intelligence level.[2]

The ability to forgive is a part of emotional intelligence:

What anger are you holding onto in your story?

Are you developing or practicing skills that allow you to process that anger in effective ways?

---

1. Bifulco, Antonia. "Loss Trauma." *Elsevier eBooks*, 2007, pp. 612–15. https://doi.org/10.1016/b978-012373947-6.00547-x.

2. "Emotional Intelligence Test." *Psychology Today*, http://www.psychologytoday.com/us/tests/personality/emotional-intelligence-test.

Chapter Three

Finders Keepers: Mentors Facilitate Change

"A mentor is someone who allows you to see the hope inside yourself." -Oprah Winfrey

My first public mentor was Oprah. I believe she's a golden example of finding resources for success. Her life has been a public journey from poverty to guru. My loyalty to her was so strong that in 1992, I gave birth to my daughter Alina while watching the Oprah Winfrey Show (a great way to pass one of the four hours of labor). Oprah, if you are reading this, can you reboot your talk show for future moms in labor and us grandmas too?

What Oprah realized early on was that she was ready for a life different than the one she was born into. She also took ownership of changing her circumstances. While we all know the healthy, happy and rich Oprah, she has had her share of darkness. Oprah was born into emotional and physical poverty and abuse and could have stayed there. Like Maya Angelou, and her 1994 book, *Wouldn't Take Nothing for My Journey Now*, dedicated to Oprah Winfrey herself, she found a way to rise.

After years of watching her show up with authenticity and bravery, some of Oprah's fearlessness wore off on me. In 1999, in the midst of caregiving for Kevin, I was inspired enough to make a powerful video. Oprah had shared her contact information on her website and was always seeking stories of hope. Caregiving is hard, but explaining ALS and how it wreaks havoc on an entire family is even harder. So, I began filming a day in the life of Kevin, a young man living with ALS. The video was a compilation of life-dependent moments that most people didn't know existed. I took footage of me giving my husband feedings through his peg tube. I took footage of the strategic process of carefully getting him in and out of bed safely with a Hoyer lift. I had the video camera going when I read Kevin's lips to communicate after he was ventilated. I had my camera ready when Kevin tried to use one finger to control his computer mouse and was frustrated to no end. We taped two quarters tightly around his index finger to weigh it down and our ingenuity worked.

I put the footage onto a disc, hand painted the manilla envelope, and mailed it away hoping to hear from Ms. Winfrey. Although I never heard from her, the process was cathartic. I still have those discs today and can watch and hear Kevin as a result. Thank you Oprah, for showing me the hope I had inside myself. Without your humble example, there would be no powerful videos to watch every time I want a glimpse of Kevin; his humor, his strength, his journey. I wouldn't have learned how to operate a video camera or thought about submitting a documentary without your courageous example.

While Oprah inspired me to reach for the stars, my parents taught more practical skills. They taught me how to work hard, how to be polite and respectful. They taught me discipline, courage, and independence. As a child, I remember an active neighborhood. Kids ran in and out of homes, in and out of the street, and in and out of trouble. We came home late at night with scraped knees and empty bellies. Our home had no central air, so many nights I fell asleep to open windows and the lull of distant voices, people taking walks, cans being dragged to the curb, and cars moving slowly down the street.

Our home was old and rumor had it that it had been moved from one end of the street to the other. The rooms were choppy and the five of us shared one full bathroom. I grew up thinking it was perfectly normal to have sheets hanging in doorways. The sheets did their best to keep the cold air contained on sticky August days, or our feet warm during the cold winter months. We took turns monopolizing the heat register and watched our pajamas expand with warm air. A real treat.

My family is made up of doers. Who needs a hand truck to move a towering refrigerator when you have four strong uncles? As a result, I never learned to ask for help and it took me decades to realize that there are times when we really need to ask for help. I grew into a capable and self-reliant adult and those qualities, among others, landed me my very first teaching job. To this day, I thank my parents for that.

Fresh out of college, I applied for a teaching position and was interviewed by the superintendent of the school district. He appreciated my GPA, my extracurricular involvement, and the fact that I was a first-generation college graduate. But what really caught his eye is that I worked three jobs at The College of NJ or TCNJ (formerly known as Trenton State) to finance my education independent of my parents' help. He had children in college and was paying for everything.

So, while my parents did not support my formal education, they supported my informal education. Learning to figure things out is a huge part of growing personally and professionally. I've been given the nickname The Closer because I get things done, but I still struggle with accomplishing those goals with confidence.

For a majority of my life, I have never really felt smart. ADHD feels like this: I am sitting at a computer, or a meeting, and thoughts go wild. *These keys feel sticky. Her braid is crooked. There's a fly on the wall. That window needs cleaning. The clock is too loud. Did the lights get brighter?* Endless. Reading a book uninterrupted, taking a test, having a conversation at a wedding, feels nearly impossible under such conditions.

People can think that you are smart. People can think that you are kind. People can value who you are and what you bring to the table, but none of that matters if you don't agree. For decades, I didn't agree. While I didn't feel smart, ADHD never kept me from succeeding, I just had to try harder. I am the perfect overachiever.

While I doubted myself, high school offered my first mentors; the first people who understood my thirst for knowledge: teachers, parents, and classmates. Ironically it was my high school friend's mom Barbara, who saw to it that her seven children graduated from college, who made sure I applied as well.

I believe it takes courage to be yourself and to maintain authenticity when you are different. My high school village of support guided me to learn about college: applications, books, clothing, meals. I had no idea where to begin. The entire process felt a little less daunting when I could talk through it with people who had done it. Still, I was scared, worried, and insecure about going to college. I know that I wasn't the only one who felt that way back then and even today. We all need mentors at every stage of our journey, especially when doing something new.

When I was first building Hope Loves Company, a non profit I founded in 2012, I met Patrishia (Trish) Cooper and immediately loved her. She had real confidence. She never went to college, but got herself a real-life education by being curious and eager to try new things. She was creative, smart, direct, and determined. I was volunteering to run a women's group called Believe, Inspire, Grow (B.I.G.), and Trish came to one of my meetings. I ran the group for many reasons: I met new people, I learned new things, I found new resources and I gained accountability. Sidenote: volunteering opens doors!

Trish was a bold redhead who, along with her daughter Carrie, invented a product called Zatswho: a set of six soft photo recognition flashcards for young children. She was older than me and she was owning her age, her intentions, and her hopes and dreams. She was a force, and I have an infinity for strong women who live the life they preach. For whatever reason, Trish took me under her wing. She and Carrie had a small radio show in Flemington, NJ and invited me on as a guest. It was a local show and a limited audience, but it was also an hour to spend with Trish, so I said yes. During our times together, Trish reminded me to own my talents and abilities by both using and sharing them. I undervalued my own compassion, leadership, and innovation as assets, and she noticed.

A few years later, Trish and her husband Paul retired to a brand-new home in North Carolina. I will never forget the day she called me out of the blue to tell me low and behold, she'd received a position as an adjunct at Lenoir-Rhyne College and asked if I would speak to her class. We discussed the details and then she had something else she wanted to mention–she was serving on the TEDx committee and wanted two of her friends to apply. I was one of those lucky friends. Let's pause right there. Here I am, in my late forties, nominated for a TEDx. Never in my wildest, boldest dreams did I believe that would happen to me.

When a door opens, when someone believes in you, you allow yourself to rise to the occasion. You take the chance with everything you have.

I read and reread the TEDx Hickory committee guidelines and process. I submitted a video. I made an outline of my topic. I practiced within the time parameters. Everything that the TEDx committee requested, I did to the best of my ability. I was scheduled to give my TEDx on November, 18th, 2017. And then sad news. On September 8, 2017 at the age of fifty-seven, Patricia Cooper died suddenly in her home.

No one had expected this news. No one was prepared, not her husband, her children, her grandchildren, nor me. My first thought was, how can I possibly do this without her in the audience? I felt shocked, sad, and unsure about moving forward. For a day or two, I wasn't sure if I would be able to deliver my talk. Suddenly, I didn't feel capable or worthy. Then I thought about Trish and who she was and who she helped me to become. Not only was I going to deliver my TEDx, but I was going to dedicate it to her. I would channel my grief and do my best to make her husband Paul proud. My husband Benton and I came in a day early to visit Asheville and the surrounding areas. We went to see the house that Paul and Trish had built together. The house was not only beautiful, it was a gallery of Trish's talents. Every detail was perfect. The blue, green and tan hues were soft and inviting. The decor was traditional yet cozy, Trish even had a room for all of her creative endeavors. I wouldn't have changed anything about their dream house. It was my dream house too, except that it was missing Trish.

In November, 2017 I delivered my TEDx in Hickory, North Carolina. As promised, I dedicated my talk to my friend.[1] I acknowledged her husband Paul in the audience and I hope that I made them both proud. During our two days in Hickory, we were spoiled. There were delicious dinners and cupcakes adorned with the TEDx logo. We got to share wine with the other speakers and watch each practice. To this day, giving a TEDx was one of the most influential and transformative experiences of my life. It happened because one woman believed in me and I believed in her.

All of the speakers were great, but one immediately got my attention and respect. He too was different. He arrived in blue jeans, sneakers, and a blue long-sleeved t-shirt, completely comfortable and relatable. He wore a hat atop his curly hair. While I could tell that he was successful, I felt his compassion and authenticity too. When he spoke, I listened. His name is Jesse Itzler.[2] I had no clue who he was, but then again, I didn't know many people in the speaking circuit. I soon learned that Jesse is an entrepreneur, speaker, endurance athlete, and the founder of Build Your Life Resume and All Day Running Club. He got his big break when he sold his company Marquis Jet to Warren Buffett in 2010, and partnered with Zico Coconut Water which he sold to Coca-Cola in 2013. Jesse gave his talk on the Happiness Meter.[3]

I have lived long enough to understand that life is full of surprises and many of them bring pure joy. A part of me believes that Trish somehow knew that I was going to need a mentor and so handpicked Jesse for me. For whatever reason, I was meant to be at the TEDx Hickory and I needed to meet Jesse.

I have had the pleasure of meeting Jesse a few times and what impresses me more than his entrepreneurial accolades are his roles as a husband, father, and son. I have since signed up for everything that Jesse and his team have offered as well as met entrepreneurs from all over the world through his platform, Build Your Life Resume. This brings me to you. If you don't have a mentor, find one. If you admire someone, let them know. Charles Caleb Colton said, "*Imitation is the sincerest form of flattery.*" It's ok to adopt the positive qualities of successful people.

In addition to Oprah, Trish, and Jesse, I'm beyond grateful to know many people who have guided my professional path. Another is Dave Howell, a dear friend, speaker and a coach. For years, out of his kindness, he has been one of my biggest supporters. While I believe that our faiths connected us, our mindsets have continued to nurture our relationship and keep us tight. Through his talent as a mentor and coach, Dave first helped me to grow the mission of Hope Loves Company, then our team, and more recently, my business, JOA SPEAKS ON. If you are just beginning the journey of your lifetime, the one you have dreamt for yourself, find a mentor. Why? Because they show you new options. We are creatures of habit and left to our own devices, we will do the same things again and again, hoping for different results. If you want a different outcome, you need a different perspective and strategy.

Mentors help you to change your behaviors and habits so that you get better results. They hold you accountable and keep you on track. They help you understand that accepting help allows you to grow in new ways. If you think everything you'll accomplish will be easy, think again. If you think that you'll never fail, think again. If you think you'll never send an email that you desperately want to retract, think again. We all need to change things about our behaviors and attitude. Mentors lead the way.

I came up with the **CHANGE** acronym to help you remember why you need a mentor.

Mentors will help you to:

CHOOSE HOPE

HARNESS YOUR STRENGTHS, KNOW YOUR CHALLENGES

ADDRESS STRATEGIC GOALS

NAVIGATE YOUR RESOURCES

GATHER POSITIVE PEOPLE

ENERGIZE YOUR MISSION

You start by choosing hope and looking at the positives of your experiences. Harness your strengths and prepare to use them. Think about your challenges, and who you can talk to about those challenges when you can't find answers, so that you can address strategic goals. If you don't have a plan, it's nearly impossible to make progress.

Create a list of the material and intellectual resources you have and research new ones available to you. Ask for help from the mentors in your life. When you are struggling, reach out to the people who you like, trust and admire. Seek guidance from positive people. Once you have direction, energize your mission. You've made an adjustment to activate the changes taking place, so take action. Even positive change can be scary or daunting. Believe in yourself and recognize your courage to address all types of change. If you don't have the money yet to sign up for mentoring and coaching programs, check out S.C.O.R.E.[4] Before you have your first session with your dedicated mentor, ask yourself these questions:

What are your greatest talents? What are your challenges?

Are you willing to make the commitment to be accountable to your goals and dreams? Do you have a business plan or are you starting from scratch?

Are you willing to take the action steps necessary to establish or scale your business?

I did not have a SCORE volunteer until my early fifties and I could not imagine my life without my incredible mentor Fred Weber. I continually count on him to guide my options and decisions as I forge ahead in my speaking and coaching career. I meet montly with him because he has the experience and fortitude I seek.

Look into SCORE and additional mentoring opportunities listed in this article.

The article reviews some of the resourceful benefits of having a mentor. Mentors provide accountability, they provide support and validation when setting goals and they increase your network and tools by sharing theirs.

Questions to consider:

What is your biggest goal right now?

What is impeding your progress?

Who are your mentors?

What guidance are you seeking from them? Could you benefit from more than one mentor?

Noteworthy:

If you have a local mentor in mind, send a hand-written card to express your admiration and interest. People like to know that their work matters. Your initiative may get a favorable response and if it doesn't, you'll still gain confidence from the experience.

---

1. O'Donnell-Ames, Jodi. "Living a Life With Purpose." *TED Talks*, http://www.ted.com/talks/jodi_o_donnell_ames_living_a_life_with_purpose.

2. "Jesse Itzler | Entrepreneur. Author. Endurance Athlete."*Jesse Itzler*, http://jesseitzler.comjesseitzler.com.

3. Itzler, Jesse. "The Happiness Meter." *TED Talks*, http://www.ted.com/talks/jesse_itzler_the_happiness_meter.

4. "Home Page." *SCORE*, http://www.score.org.

Chapter Four

Finding Resources: The Importance of Curiosity and Learning

"Human resources are like natural resources: they are often buried deep. You have to go looking for them; they are not just lying around on the surface." -Ken Robinson

Minerals are one of our greatest resources, but they are often found far below what we can see on the surface. I've found personal growth resources to be the same way. Life has taught me that if you dig deep enough–if you stay hungry, curious, and authentic–you will attract truly supportive people into your life and those who can guide your way to the resources you need.

Listen. Learn. As you find your way, don't forget to reciprocate that mentoring when you become a resourced light yourself.

I have always been curious, and I find many things fascinating. If I had the means when I was a child, I would have purchased every book and taken every extracurricular class I could.

The first time I took a class outside of public school was in college. I remember how hard it was to choose my electives when they were all so enticing. You mean I only get one? When I became an adult and had a teaching job, I got to sign up for a class that interested me. I was twenty-six years old when I signed up for an improvisational acting class. I don't even know if I knew what the word improvisational meant at that time, but it was inexpensive and sounded fun.

While I'd been in college and had some sense of the broader world around me, I knew that there was still so much more to learn. What was life like outside of the U.S.? How did the internet work? What would it be like to be on a real stage? One night, my acting teacher was demonstrating how to project our voices and articulate properly when he mentioned three letters that improved my communication skills tremendously: NPR, National Public Radio. I'd never heard of NPR, but he suggested we listen to improve our speaking skills. First rule of personal growth is to try what those who're where you want to be, suggest. So, as soon as I hopped into my car that night after class, I tuned into 90.9 FM, Philadelphia, NPR for me.

NPR opened up my world in a way that I never thought possible. It was a direct source, at my disposal, for creative, intelligent, funny, and relevant information. I quickly became engulfed in the programs and stories that accompanied my car rides. If I arrived at my destination and the story's resolution was within reach, I sat in the car listening intently (there is an actual term for this phenomena: driveway moments!) or ran into the house and found it on the computer. I gave my first public radio donation dialing in from my cell phone, from my car, enraptured by the storytelling, tears in my eyes, and a grateful heart for access to such literary wealth. Have you ever walked into a party suggesting an episode of The Pulse, This American Life or Fresh Air before you even said hello? NPR is still my number one go-to on long rides. I learned about this new resource because I stepped outside of my comfort zone, I took a new class, met new people, and took the advice of one teacher.

Today, there is a plethora of information at your disposal. There are also more than 2 million podcasts offering a diverse array of content to entertain and educate through storytelling and interviews. I have enjoyed podcasts so much that I decided to host my own, Gratitude to Latitude, and soon realized that I had enough people to interview in my immediate circle. I created a way to not only highlight my amazing connections, but also learn from their experiences. My podcast granted quality time with more than two dozen fascinating influential people. I listened to every word and put their knowledge into action.

I can't mention helpful resources without my friend Dr. Lawrence Nespoli, whom I've known for nearly ten years. An equally enthusiastic student for life, Larry and I share many similarities. We are perpetual students, we love to exercise, we are both, dare I admit, adorably nerdy. Our children, who first dated a decade ago, coined us two peas in a pod. In 2022, I invited Larry on my podcast to talk about his work in education. Like me, Larry is of the age that he should, theoretically, be slowing down. We're grandparents now, but there's no sign of owning retirement in either of our lives. I don't think we will ever stop doing the things we love, and our professional goals are a healthy part of those things.

Larry is an unstoppable vision of optimism. He's the "mayor" that everyone in town loves and respects. He wants everyone to have access to a college degree. He wants everyone to be successful. He wears his title, Dr. of Education, with great pride, yet he does so in a humble and nonchalant manner. Just as Dr. Nespoli supports his students, there is someone who wants to see you succeed, where you are. In every institution of learning, there is at least one dedicated and caring advocate for your best interest. In high school, I met two women who provided both the emotional and professional support I needed to begin the road to college. When I felt I had no options, they opened the door for me. If it weren't for them, I would not have taken that path. I thank them still.

Do the research and the legwork. Scour the web, read, use free programs at the library, and find a way. Part of growing means being open to learning new things. Learning new things results in possibilities and therefore, hope. When I needed answers, I found affordable and reliable resources. So will you.

As someone who had little means to go to college, I asked Larry how to get an education without the traditional resources in place.

"I'm passionate about community colleges. They are there for you. Education is the great equalizer in terms of economic mobility and promoting equity in our society. Your local community college is a great door to knock on, and they might point you to other options. There are many good-paying technical jobs that require some college, but not a bachelor's degree.

Think about nursing, think about information technology programs, and business technologies. You can stop along the way to work for several years with a nursing degree or with an IT degree of some kind."

You can take your time.

When my children were thinking about college, I suggested that they start at community colleges. There are as many incentives for that path as there are for a four-year degree.

If getting an education is part of your challenges, start asking questions. Surround yourself with people who made it happen. Go to networking meetings. Join a mastermind group. Sign up for Meetup. Someone will have suggestions for you. There are countless grants out there too. It will take time and energy to find those grants, but it's worth it.[1]

Dr. Nespoli's guidance is a reminder that there are many ways to advance your education.

How many of us really know what we want to be when we grow up, by the time we are seventeen? I began my career as a teacher. While I am not teaching in a school system today, my college education and experiences in teaching have been the foundation for every career choice I've since made. Everything I learned in college continues to serve me well. If college is not for you, you have options, including trade schools and apprenticeships. If you are just starting or considering switching careers, I recommend taking a personality test to help you evaluate which careers are best for you where you are right now.[2] Your interests and goals will likely change with the years.

I had enough money to apply to one college and did, thinking my chances were slim.

When my acceptance letter arrived in the mail I was over the moon. Next challenge: how? I hit a wall. I began digging for resources. By the time I was seventeen, I had saved a whopping $1,000 dollars by working five jobs from paper routes to fixing subs at my grandparents' deli. Since I'd wanted to become a teacher, I consulted with a teacher who suggested that I apply for a few scholarships. When a door opens, you walk through it.

The scholarship money was enough to seal the deal. I was heading to what was then Trenton State to study Early Childhood Education and English. I could have used one of Dr. Nespoli's pep talks back then–it's a universal reminder for all of us who are working towards a big goal.

"Listen, I promise you, you may be an exception to this rule, but there are a few exceptions. At some time in this journey, you will wake up one day and be convinced that this was a terrible mistake. The single most important thing that will determine whether you get to the finish line and graduate is your grit and your perseverance."

Believe it or not, getting accepted into college, or another program, or even landing a dream job, is not the hardest part. The real work begins when the daily commitment kicks in. When you are required to show up, ready to engage and learn. When you must prepare for tests, meetings, and challenges that are not yet in your skillset. As Dr. Nespoli shared, I too believe that grit and perseverance are instrumental in the success of our long-term commitments. Good news is that you can build both. Bad news (at first) is that the practice is ongoing.

Like most people, I had to work on building my grit, perseverance and mindset. It's human nature to gravitate towards comfort exclusively, that's why there are heated seats in cars, microwaves, and riding lawn mowers. It's interesting though, the easier our lives get, the harder it is to maintain grit. The objective is not just about overcoming an obstacle. It's about the confidence obtained from knowing you can do hard things. If you are out of touch with building grit, listen to other stories of hard-won success. Nearly every night, I fall asleep to a self-help podcast, meditation, or a gritty story. Today more than ever, you have access to information that can provide the resources and direction needed for professional and personal improvement. They will broaden your knowledge, open your mind, and encourage action.

Resources won't simply come to you, however. You need to go to them, and the people who know of their existence.

Questions to consider:

What resources shared above can you put into immediate use?

What resources will you continue to research?

Which ones might you share with others?

Noteworthy:

Create a list of grants, scholarships and funding opportunities and weigh your options. Listen to podcasts and read books by those who inspire you.

Brainstorm your big dreams with trusted friends who believe in you.

---

1. "Grants." *Grants*, http://www.sba.gov/funding-programs/grants.

2. "Free Personality Test | 16Personalities." *16Personalities*, http://www.16personalities.com/free-personality-test.

Chapter Five

Grinding the Grit Muscle and the Importance of Perseverance

"You can go a month without food, you can live three days without water, but you can't go more than sixty seconds without hope."
-*Sean Swarner*

The word hope takes up as much space in my heart as the word love. Long before my nonprofit, Hope Loves Company was even a thought, I valued the word Hope. Having been born on Christmas Day, it was one of the names my parents considered for me. Hope would have been a great namesake. Emily Dickinson's poem, *Hope is the Thing With Feathers*, was introduced to me in college. It has remained one of my favorite poems and soothed me on the roughest days. After Kevin's death, I worked at the ALS Hope Foundation. In my late thirties, I moved to Hopewell, NJ. I have been surrounded and embraced in hope all my life. Hope will always be the anchor in my daily efforts and the catalyst in my progress. I choose to live my life's purpose in all that I do.

I have seen people who've faced enormous challenges without hope and it's incredibly hard to watch. When I heard about Sean Swarner, I knew I had to learn more about him. Sean is the physical and emotional essence of hope and he agreed to be a guest on my podcast. To prepare for our interview, I watched his documentary, *True North* and soon grabbed the tissues.

Sean first battled cancer when he was only thirteen years old, and was told he had three months to live. At the age of sixteen, cancer struck again. Sean was told he had fourteen days to live. He was placed in a medically-induced coma for a year. Somehow, he survived the ordeal and regained his strength with the goal that began by crawling eight feet from his hospital bed to the bathroom.[1]

Sean's story has captivated audiences all over the world. He is the first cancer survivor to stand on top of the world, on Mt. Everest. He then went on to climb the highest peaks in Africa, Europe, South America, North America, Australia, and Antarctica, thus completing the "7-Summits." As if that wasn't enough, and with only one functioning lung, Sean skied both the South and the North Poles, earning the revered and coveted honor of the Explorer's Grand Slam Award. His mindset took incredible work to build.

"I've worked on my mental muscles. I also tapped into what fuels me, I've tapped into a certain purpose in my life. I think that purpose gives me passion. With that passion, I derive meaning. So, I think underlying everything I do is fully knowing what my personal core values are, because once I know what my core values are, I can utilize those to find my purpose, my passion."

Sean founded a non-profit, Cancer Climber, which encourages cancer patients, survivors and their caregivers to conquer Everest. Having the privilege of interviewing Sean meant that I got to hear this directly from him. We can learn a lot from anomalies directly, they reveal more about us, and how much more we can achieve than we may believe we can.

"I'm the only person in history to climb Everest, the highest mountain on every continent, ski to both the North and South poles, and complete the Hawaii Ironman in their lifetime.

However, I did it. I was once given 14 days to live. I was read my last rights. I was in a medically-induced coma for a year in my life. I see things a little bit differently than most people. I am more afraid of not living than I am living. I really wish more people would understand that this isn't a dress rehearsal we're going through in life. Numerous times throughout the year, I get a piece of paper and lay it horizontally. Draw a horizontal line across it. Draw two vertical lines at the end of that horizontal line. At the left side, put the four digit year that you were born. Add roughly 80 years to that. Write down that four digit number at the end of that line. That's your life line."

This activity brings reality to light. Time is finite, yet we don't typically think of it so logically. Our lifeline is what's printed in our obituaries. Yet, how many of us really think about what we want our lives to look like and how we use that time? Sean's story got me thinking about how we handle adversity and challenges. I have met people who give up after the first try and I know others who have failed ten times and rise again. But why? Grit is the answer. According to Dr. Angela Duckworth, "The secret to outstanding achievement is not talent but a special blend of passion and persistence," which she calls "grit." [2]

She explains that when you increase your resilience, you ultimately increase your grit. Why is that the case? Resilience is the ability to bounce back from adversity. The more that we are able to recover, the higher our chances for staying on track and reaching our goals. The Merriam-Webster definition of grit is *courageously persistent*. The online dictionary also gives a further explanation that grit's origin stems from Middle English for sand and gravel. Grit has been around since before the 12th century, but the first appearance of gritty in print in English was near the end of the 16th century, when it was used in the sense of "resembling or containing small hard granules." Grit entered American slang by the end of the 19th century to capture its meaning today.[3]

First and foremost, get a copy of *Grit* by Dr. Duckworth and devour every word. Then read it again. Through the pages, she concentrates on the four elements of grit: interest, practice, purpose, and hope. You can work on improving these characteristics to have more grit. While I valued interest, practice, and purpose, I especially appreciate the inclusion of the word hope. I recently read an article describing the discovery that hope was a significantly stronger predictor of mental health than was mental illness.[4] Read that again. Hope is greater than DNA. If you feel that you are less than gritty, there are many people who have shared daily habits to strengthen the grit factor. If you want to get grittier, you might have to do things out of your comfort zone. While it feels great to wake up at seven, set your alarm for five now and then.

Work on a project, exercise, read, or do something you normally wouldn't do at that or any hour. You can leave the comfort of your warm bed before your alarm goes off. You can do gritty things.

Wim Hoff, a Dutch motivational speaker and extreme athlete, believes in the power of cold-water therapy. After reading about his cold habits, I turned my comfortable hot showers into periodic cold showers. I can't say I like cold showers one bit, but I survive them and feel refreshed and empowered afterwards. You can do gritty things.

This brings me back to a powerful question: what impact did Sean's hope and grit have on his recovery? Everything. Sean's hope kept him climbing and he's now helping others do the same at Cancer Climber Association. Part of the delight of surrounding yourself with those you admire is the ability to learn from the mindsets of individuals like Sean, who ask the tough questions and seek answers.

Questions to Consider:

Do you believe in hope?

What is your mindset on a daily basis?

How do you cultivate a life full of hope and promise?

Pain, loss, challenges will happen. What healthy tools do you use to address the tough times?

Noteworthy:

When it comes to getting things done, change your wording from, "I have to" to "I get to."

Every morning, write three things for which you are grateful. Each night, reflect on something that you accomplished that made you stronger or grittier.

---

1. "True North: The Sean Swarner Story." *True North: The Sean Swarner Story*, http://www.truenorthdocfilm.com.

2. Duckworth, Angela L. *Grit: The Power of Passion and Perseverance*. 2016, http://pusin.ppm-manajemen.ac.id/index.php?p=show_detail&id=48064&keywords=.

3. "Grit | Etymology, Origin and Meaning of Grit by Etymonline." *Etymonline*, http://www.etymonline.com/word/grit.

4. Venning, Anthony, et al. "Is Hope or Mental Illness a Stronger Predictor of Mental Health?" *The International Journal of Mental Health Promotion*, vol.13, no.2, Taylor and Francis, Dec. 2011, pp. 32–39. https://doi.org/10.1080/14623730.2011.9715654

Chapter Six

Rule of Threes: Clarity of Purpose and Priorities

"In order to get something done, you have to get started."
-George Anthony

Anything that requires change, requires work. There's no way around that. Anything that requires work, demands action. Sometimes, just the thought of the process is enough to stop us in our tracks. That's why new year's resolutions typically don't last.

We write down our goals for the new year and our vision ends on a piece of paper, in a notebook, atop a desk in a messy pile of papers.

In 2006, I was raising three compassionate children, Nora, Adam and Alina, who had all suffered the same trauma. As young children, nearly the age of my granddaughter now, they had lost a parent to ALS. They watched, with little understanding, as a healthy and active parent, become wheelchair bound and unable to speak. I can't imagine how that felt for them. It was unbearable for me and I had awareness of ALS and its progression. I was doing my best to provide the resources I'd learned in my teacher training, but I was still grieving too. I needed additional help. So, I started calling schools and therapists, to ask about children and loss as the result of ALS.

We were a new family full of love and hope, yet we still had a cloud of grief over us and it sometimes poured down on us. I remember calling the local library to ask them about books for children about grief. There were a few, but the content was too young for our children who were smart and curious, who needed more.

So few in my new circle knew of ALS, how it progresses, the changes and trauma it causes families or that it was even terminal. So, I continued to do my best to wrestle through it and that's when it hit me. What if I started a nonprofit that focuses on this one thing? Helping children who love someone with ALS?

It has always been curious to me how certain people get things done when, at our core, we are all basically working with the same tools: our time, our skills, and our resources. I know one man whose daily life depends on his resolutions. His name is George Anthony. George is a former teacher, conflict resolution specialist, mentor and the Primary United Nations Representative for the NGO, Pathways to Peace. His interview was different from most of the others for one reason, his work stems from social injustice. Just thinking of the words social injustice causes me anxiety. It's systemic and everywhere and the work that needs to be done is overwhelming. I like solving problems. I like checking off lists. I like seeing the fruition of my work. George and his team are tackling issues that are bigger and older than all of us.

Still, George is fueled by hope. At the time of our interview in 2021, this book wasn't a thought. I was simply enjoying learning from the people who moved me. The people who consistently demonstrated how to be extraordinary humans. The word hope came up so frequently during our conversation, I had to share Mr. Anthony's words with you.

"Everything I do is towards hope. In order to get something done, you have to begin. If you put an obstacle in my way, that obstacle isn't there to stop me. The obstacle is there to teach me. We learn from our struggles."

Imagine if we all looked at obstacles in the confines of his words. Like George, I strongly believe in the power to create something beautiful out of our struggles. Hope Loves Company, something beautiful, would be birthed out of loss. I reflected on my past and planned a brighter direction, one that would result in something greater than me. I found another quote and added it to my desk. "I always wondered why someone didn't do something about that. Then I realized, "I am someone." unknown

Hope. Loves. Company. The words slipped off my tongue with ease. The uncompromising opposite of the expression "misery loves company." I saw a flash of children. I saw hugs. I saw activities that would be both fun and educational. I saw free supportive resources. I called my girlfriend Linda Cassidy and shared my vision. She loved the idea and was onboard. I had a long conversation with my husband Benton too because this vision would take a team, time and our entire house as a temporary office space. We had some understanding of what would be involved. Hard work. Long hours. Rejection. Fundraising. Disappointment.

Progress. One day, success. Yet, he too was on board. He had no idea what he was getting into.

When you start a non-profit from your dining room table, you don't dine at that table.

You work, dream, and strategize at that table. Our dining room table was adorned not with plates and centerpieces, but with papers: mission statements, tax exempt applications, and lists of possible board members.

Really, I had no idea what I was getting into either. I was surfing the web one day when I came across a 2021 article highlighting a study by the University of Scranton, which found that 92% of people fail to achieve their goals.[1] That's a pretty big percentage. It causes us to ask the question, "Why?" Daily commitment is hard, but it's necessary to succeed. That's why there are thousands of books on the topic of finding and achieving success.

While staying on track is tough, people do it. 8% of them. Products like Method, AirBnB and Spanx weren't successful overnight. If we don't read about their journeys, we only see the end results, the successful products or ideas making entrepreneurs rich. There is so much more to learn from their journeys to the top. The grit, energy, sweat, and failure that went into their success. From my perspective, I thought the most difficult part of starting a non-profit would be the initial legwork: the legal paperwork, the registrations, finding and training a board of directors, and seeking funding. Not even close. The real challenge came with the first list of big goals and a limited bank account. I spent many hours at the library. I read books about having a growth mindset: *Think and Grow Rich* by Napoleon Hill, *How to Win Friends and Influence People* by Dale Carnegie, *The Four Agreements* by Don Miguel Ruiz, *How Successful People Think* by John C. Maxwell, *The Seven Habits of Highly Effective People* by Steve Covey, *Think Again* by Adam Grant, and more. I read *Non-Profits for Dummies*, (in a corner of the library, away from others because I already felt dumb enough).

To the general public, starting a business or nonprofit is exciting. No doubt it can be.

But right there in the library, my nose in a book and my jaw to the floor, it hit me. *What have I done? How will I grow this idea into a legitimate and sustainable organization? What do I know about starting a business?* Nothing. What most people don't know is the truth. When you start a nonprofit, or a for profit business, you give birth to an idea and a vision that is, ultimately, your responsibility for life. If you aren't ready to commit to the long-term marathon, your patience, stamina, and integrity will be tested. You sign your name to every legal paper, every contract, and non-disclosure agreement. If you don't have an office, your home address is the office. If you don't have the initial funds or equity, you are the equity.

Eventually, as I went to non-profit meetings, listened to the experts, asked questions, and found answers, I learned more. I let go of fear. I trusted myself as well as the process. I felt empowered to move forward. So how did I grow Hope Loves Company- the only non profit in the U.S. dedicated to supporting children and young adults who've had or have a loved one in their lives battling ALS? Slowly. One day at a time. In threes, without fail, every single day. I did three things to move the needle forward. These were three priorities. Three non-negotiables. Three, I don't care if I am sick, tired, or sick and tired, these must happen today.

The first priority was to do something to spread awareness of our mission. That meant posting on social media. It meant pictures and quotes and putting the reality of ALS in front of people. It meant sharing the stories of the caregiving children I'd met too, including my own. I reached out to journalists on H.A.R.O (Help a Reporter Out, now Cision Connectivity), the news desks of Philly stations, and anyone who included the three letters ALS in my line of sight. We didn't have an office. We didn't have a dedicated HLC phone number. All inquiries came to me on my flip phone.

I can still clearly remember a call I got one beautiful beach day at the New Jersey shore, with my family on vacation. When you're an entrepreneur, there is no true vacation. I answered the phone and was immediately met with a panic-stricken mother of three. I walked away from the beach to a quiet, isolated spot where I could listen to her closely and be present to her needs. She had been recently diagnosed with ALS and wanted guidance on how to explain ALS to her children. I made her a promise and two days later, when I was home, I put a copy of my book, *The Stars that Shine*, in the mail to her. I enclosed a brochure about HLC and a reminder to call me when she received her copy.

Today, we have access to just about anyone through social media. So, I did my research. I learned about celebrities or public figures who were somehow connected to ALS and I took a chance and reached out. They may have starred in a movie that touched on the topic of ALS. They may have walked in a fundraiser to support ALS. It didn't matter. My hope was that they would learn more about our unique mission, follow us, like us, contact us, and eventually donate. I used LinkedIn, Facebook, Twitter, Ticktok and Instagram to get the word out.

The second thing I did each day was to focus on increasing our net worth. I searched for other ALS nonprofit organizations, grantors, philanthropists, and volunteers. We needed everyone to pitch in and offer their skills, connections, and money. I created a list of organizations devoted to supporting children, the terminally ill, or caregivers, then, one by one, sent letters and donation requests. I also began applying for grants and aimed to complete one application per month.

The third thing I did each day was connect with families facing ALS. On every social media platform, I typed ALS in the search bar. That led me to families with children. Connecting was my purpose. Helping others was my purpose. Sharing my goals and letting them know that I was here for them fueled my purpose to succeed. It was a form of manifesting and outreach.

These calls were made daily, each one more difficult than the last. One person asked me out right, "You lost your husband Kevin to ALS years ago. Why do you remain in this fight? How do you do it emotionally, day in and day out?" I paused and then responded. "Because there were so many people there for us. We were surrounded by love and help during our darkest days. We needed help and now, people need me."

Hope Givers are everywhere. During the six years that Kevin battled ALS, I learned so much. I learned to be more patient, grateful, and calm. I learned to be humble and to forgive. I learned to be a nurse and to operate a ventilator. But the greatest lessons were from other families who had faced ALS too. These families taught us ALS life hacks that simplified our daily activities. When Kevin could no longer lift his arms for us to change his shirt, we learned to cut the shirt down the back and put it on from the front. When Kevin's fingers started to curl, we learned to roll up a washcloth and use it to support his hands and keep his finger straight.

These were practical, life-changing ideas ascertained purely through hands-on experience. Right from the source. Starting Hope Loves Company was a means to be a resource to others as dozens had been to me. To be a Hope Giver too.

Distractions are a dime a dozen. They interrupt your goals and rob you of your focus, so prepare yourself. Turn off the noise of everything else vying for your attention. Mute the phone. Close your tabs on your computer and in your brain. Focus on only the priority tasks that will make an immediate impact; a palpable difference and noticeable progress to gear you up for the next goal.

Warren Buffet has shared some guidance on how to really focus on goals. He created the 5/25 rule. Here's how it works: You write down the top 25 things you need to accomplish to move forward with your life's dreams. He then suggests you put them in order of importance.

Once you've done that, the top five are your focus and the other twenty are temporarily put out of existence. This way, you are exclusively focused on your top five goals. Just forget the other 20? Yes, for now. It's not easy to do, but it's effective.

As a part of my reading, I also learned about Jim Rohn. Jim Rohn was a hope giver. He was an entrepreneur, speaker, and author. He grew up in Idaho in poverty. But everything changed when he learned to manifest his dream life. He became a millionaire by the age of thirty. He first started speaking for free via the Rotary Club. His first topic was aptly named, *Idaho Farm Boy Makes It*. He got my attention. Jim had a great work ethic and mentor, Earl Shoaff, an American Entrepreneur and Speaker, who took him under his wing. They both were extremely successful in life. That didn't stop Jim from being broke by his mid-thirties. Yet he overcame those challenges, and rose to millionaire status again. He suggests these steps: practice self-preparation, be ready for opportunities, and list your three most important long-term goals.

No one person can grow a non-profit alone. Family and friends offered their time and talents. My sister-in-law Keiren Dunfee raised her hand and designed our wonderful logo. She captured the essence of my vision in one image, with little direction. Our Board of Directors contributed information, guidance, and countless valuable volunteer hours. Families affected by ALS made donations and grantors started to know our name. Organizations reached out to thank us for our work. Slowly, everything started to fall in place and HLC began to feel like a real entity. Progress is possible when you are ready to ask for help, learn everything you can, and take it one day at a time. The world is made up of dreamers and doers: the only difference is that the doers take action. Most people's dreams end when a need for consistent action begins. That's why we depend on mentors, coaches, and our fearless five (more in Chapter 7) to keep us accountable.

Getting started matters and so does staying in the game.

Questions to consider:

What process are you taking to get focused? How are you best using your time each day? What are the distractions in your life?

How will you stay on track?

Have you tried the rule of threes or the 25/5 rule? Are you ready to add them to your plan?

Noteworthy:

Go to meetup.com and see if there are leadership groups gathering near you

Join LinkedIn and start connecting and growing your network. There are many other free professional communities as well.

---

1. Diamond, Dan. "Just 8% of People Achieve Their New Year's Resolutions. Here's How They Do It." *Forbes*, 1 Jan. 2013, http://www.forbes.com/sites/dandiamond/2013/01/01/just-8-of-people-achieve-their-new-years- resolutions-heres-how-they-did-it/?sh=2791022d596b.

Chapter Seven

Finding your Fearless Five: The Power of Learning from Others

"Anything or anyone who does not bring you alive is too small for you." -David Whyte

For years, a small handwritten quote sat on my desk. I don't recall where I first saw the quote, or when. I had no idea who David Whyte was, but I knew his words had power. So, I scribbled his quote on paper and taped it in plain sight. I learned that Mr. Whyte is a poet, writer, and internationally acclaimed speaker. His quote did something huge for me. It made me think about the people in my life. It reminded me daily to think big, not small. It reminded me that Hope Loves Company and I were two different entities. We both needed different things to survive.

Thank you, Mr. Whyte, for your wisdom. I gave that quote some thought and I took action. At our core, we are energy, like everything else in the universe. Each day things, people, ideas, and events will affect that energy. We can choose, at any given time, to connect with our energy and what inspires our momentum. Life gets interesting when you start thinking about what that energy looks like, and how you want to keep your flame going.

Creating something bigger than me required enormous energy. As a founder, I jumped out of bed every morning. I had plans, lists, calls, and passion to fill each day. Most days, I didn't think to eat or brush my teeth until the afternoon. I was absorbed in my vision and so focused that my life/work balance wasn't. I was driven to bring HLC to fruition, even if it meant cavities. Everything about creating HLC brought me alive. It encompassed every skill I had: writing, leading, creating, teaching, coaching, and more.

Of course, there are important aspects of life not in this category that are essential to being a good human. Going to the hospital to visit a sick friend does not bring me alive, but it does feel good to hold the hand of a friend who needs me. Picking up litter on the street does not bring me alive but it's the right thing to do. Putting my cart back at the grocery store does not bring me alive but it saves cars from door dings. You get the idea. There is a difference in our conscious intention and that difference is huge.

As a sensitive person, I feel and absorb energy all around me. I need to know who's in the room with me. I need to prepare myself if the energy will deplete me. Take notice if you feel tired or energized when you leave someone's house. When you make a conscious decision to spend more time with the people who fuel you, you have more time for the things that bring you alive.

A year or two into the formation of HLC, I decided to emulate five people whose journeys were what I imagined for mine. In my mind, I gave them a name, my Fearless Five. They were entrepreneurs. Leaders. Game changers. Their habits brought lessons to mine, and I soon felt empowered. My Five were a mix of personalities, abilities, vocations, and relationships. At any time, they were both willing and able to push me out of my comfort zone and remind me that I had valuable work to do. While I wasn't always the most appreciative receiver, I learned from each experience. If you want to do hard things, you have to do the hard work. If you want a unique outcome, you need a unique effort. You might need to hear things that you'd rather avoid. I remember when one of my fearless five shared I wasn't a great business person. It was true, but not what I wanted to hear before attending an important meeting and an intimidating staff.

The positive discomfort we experience while reaching for our goals–and being willing to fail at them–creates room for growth.

We need to think about our fearless five. We need to write down their names and keep them close. If they are in your circle, spend more time with them. Ask them questions when it feels appropriate, and watch how they react to challenges. If they are influencers, read their books. Hear them speak, follow them on social media. The point is, learn from the examples of those you respect and admire. The key is that you believe they keep you accountable in the department of ongoing self-improvement. Jim Rohn said, "You're the average of the five people you spend most of your time with." Confucius knew this too, "If you are the smartest person in the room, you are in the wrong room." My five is ever flowing based on where I am in my journey.

I witnessed the power of the fearless five first-hand with my children and my great niece, Raquel. Raquel grew up with two parents who loved her dearly, but deeply struggled with battles of their own. On many occasions, they were limited in the support they could offer. In 2001, nearly three months to the day after losing Kevin, I got a call from Raquel's mom, my niece, Reina. She was in jail and she asked if Raquel could be in my custody. Absolutely. She was just a little over three years old.

For one year, Raquel was in my care. We read together. She went to school with my daughter, Alina. She made friends in our neighborhood. She was funny, smart, and curious. She had a bedtime. Prayers. Loving structure and routines. One early morning, I heard a lot of noise coming from the kitchen. It sounded like something dragging. Alina was asleep in bed next to me so I knew it couldn't be her. I went slowly down the steps and heard more noise. It sounded like cereal hitting the floor. When I walked into the kitchen, Raquel was enjoying a bowl of cereal. The floor was peppered with Cheerios. She had a big, proud smile on her face. She had dragged the chair to the pantry and the refrigerator and made herself some breakfast. I kissed her through teary eyes and wished her good morning. In small and important ways, Raquel knew what she needed.

One year after Raquel entered our home, when I'd requested adoption in court, she was returned to her parents. Everything had pointed to Raquel joining our little family, but I was instructed to gather Raquel's things, to pull her out of school and welcome her father in a few hours at my home. The pain and hurt that occurred that day, and months after, was like losing Kevin all over again. Raquel was gone as quickly as she came. I saw Raquel at family occasions, and whenever we could, we had visits and calls. She continued to know how much I loved her.

Seventeen years later, on December 24, 2018, Raquel called to ask if she could visit. Her call was a gift. To have her with us for our Christmas holiday was extra special. I adored her and wanted as much time with her as possible. We had an amazing Christmas Eve as a family and that evening Raquel asked if she could stay a few days. Those days turned into months. Drives to pick up more stuff. A year passed by. Then two. Three. Eventually, Raquel lived with us for more than five years. During that time, only months apart, Raquel lost both of her parents. When she lost her mom, we were on the porch enjoying the sunshine. Raquel got a call from her dad.

The glass of lemon water she was holding dropped, smashing into hundreds of pieces before Raquel dropped to her knees. Her upbringing. Her losses. Her challenges. All of that could have brought Raquel down to her knees forever, but didn't. I saw so much of myself in Raquel. She is: Determined. Continuously Curious. Adventurous. Compassionate. Independent. Strong.

Raquel matriculated to college, excelled, graduated with honors, got a fabulous job, got an apartment, and left the nest. I know that none of that was easy for her, but she made it look easy. Passion will do that. What moved me the most was the transition that took place. She read countless books. She wanted to get healthier. She organized her space and her life. She found her five people.

We can hold on to our pasts or even stay there, or we can move through our experiences and create a life that is fulfilling, and healthy. I admire Raquel for her courage to do just that. My children have all done the same. Quite honestly, I didn't raise them with many of the tools that I share in this book because I didn't have them yet. But, they have learned on their own accord.

So, how do we find your five? Years ago, I read *How to Win Friends and Influence People* by Dale Carnegie. The book is more than eighty years old, but the wisdom it contains is timeless.[1] Try these suggestions:

1. DON'T CRITICIZE.

2. GIVE HONEST AND SINCERE APPRECIATION.

3. AROUSE IN THE OTHER PERSON AN EAGER WANT.

4. TALK IN TERMS OF THE OTHER PERSON'S INTERESTS.

5. REMEMBER NAMES.

6. BECOME GENUINELY INTERESTED IN OTHER PEOPLE.

7. AVOID ARGUMENTS.

8. BE A GOOD LISTENER.

I always stay connected to my five. If you don't have your fearless five, make them a priority. Go to conferences. Pay attention at meetings. Follow those you admire and don't be afraid to reach out. Most people are honored to know that their work or perspective is appreciated.

Your Fearless Five are precious gold. Why is that? No one is born a professional. No one is born an expert. We all start somewhere. If someone is where you want to be, you can learn from them. No doubt that they have, at some point, felt completely rejected, lost, underappreciated, unqualified, and defeated. They hold resources and information that could jumpstart your success. Value them. Spent time with them. Love them. Thank them. Show up and be present. And when you walk into a room, bring the same energy, creativity and enthusiasm with you. Hope is cyclical because life is cyclical. Once you get to the place of your dreams, it's your job to be a hope giver too. When you are struggling, when you are tired, when you feel like you aren't making progress, it might be hard to value where someone else is– especially if that place is where you long to be in your life. Be careful not to be envious of someone's progress. Instead, utilize their success as a resource to learn. Ask them questions and take notes. Odds are they were once in your shoes.

Comparing journeys does nothing but encourage resentment and complacency.

Questions to consider:

Who are your fearless five?

Do you show gratitude and appreciation to them?

Who do you want to be a new contact in your life? How can you reach out? How do you show up? Are you consistent?

Will you be one of someone's five?

Noteworthy:

Practice your elevator pitch. An elevator pitch is a 30 second review of who you are, what you do and what you want to prepare for that chance meeting in the elevator or anywhere. It's one thing to know who you are and what you do, but it's an art to give a great pitch. Write it down. Practice it with a friend. Record it and improve your pitch. If you get stuck in an elevator with Tony Robbins one day, you'll be glad that you have a pitch.

---

1. Carnegie, Dale A. *How to Win Friends and Influence People*. 1936, http://ci.nii.ac.jp/ncid/BB02478846?l=en.

Chapter Eight

Dead Ant, Dead Ant: Integrating Power and Positivity Into Your Life

"When you change the way you look at things, the things you look at change." -Wayne Dyer

Perspective is everything. Wayne Dyer's words are a potent reminder that with a little tweaking, we can change our perspective and increase our hope. I remember having lunch with a friend a few months after Kevin died. It had been some time since we sat down and shared a meal together. I had a lot of catching up to do and was still learning how to matriculate back into the world as a widow. I was doing my best to be present, but then the tears started to form. My friend was going on dates and while she was nearing forty years old, wasn't sure if she'd ever been in love. She was searching.

She looked at me, handed me a tissue, held my hand and said, "*Remember how lucky you are to have felt such love. Some of us don't know what that is.*" Perspective. Getting back into a productive life meant changing my outlook. "*Hi, my name is Jodi. I am a widow and sadness pervades my soul,*" doesn't go over very well in general conversation. Even in my caregiving world, I noticed the reactions of others to my sad story. While I needed to tell it, no one wanted to hear it. So, I began by thinking about the words I used and how they were impacting both me and those around me. Until then, I hadn't considered if they were creating a positive or negative perspective. They were just words.

Instead of saying, "I have to go to work today," I now say, "I get to work today." Instead of saying, "I must do laundry," it's " I get to have clean clothes," with awareness. I couldn't believe how many times I said can't, won't, don't, shouldn't. Like most of us, I struggle with keeping a positive outlook when the cards are stacked against me. While I used to say things and not think about the language I was using, I am now aware of my word choices and the thoughts that fuel me. It begins with awareness of your own internal dialogue. Eventually, I learned to say, "*Hi, my name is Jodi. I am a non-profit founder as a result of loss, and we are doing really great things to support children.*"

Much better. So, give this some thought, have you used these phrases?

I would apply for the job, but they would never consider me. I will never be in shape.

Why bother making a new year's resolution, I won't stick to it anyway.

Be careful, your mind just might believe what you think. There's an old quote from Buddha that I love, "All that we are, is the result of what we have thought. The mind is everything. What we think, we become."[1] There are no truer words.

These days, I congratulate myself when I avoid using negative words and replace them with empowering words. Since we're talking about perspective and ways to improve ours, it's the perfect time to consider all facets of influence. How you think is important. It's also important to be aware of what you watch, hear, read, and see. You are a sponge, and you absorb everything that your five senses recognize.

A few years ago, while watching PBS, I learned about Psychiatrist and Neuroscientist Dr. Daniel Amen and his A.N.T.s. acronym. In the early 1990s, Dr. Amen coined the term, **Automatic Negative Thoughts (ANTs)** to describe the negative, gloomy, pessimistic thoughts that enter our minds. He got the idea when he arrived home from a difficult day at work to find an ant infestation in his house. The ants were invading his home, his space. While handling the pests, he made the A.N.T. analogy. Automatic Negative Thoughts are normal. They come marching in, at the most inconvenient times. Before a job interview, major tests, public speeches, or a busy day. They can wreak havoc on our confidence and fuel self-doubt, leaving us feeling inadequate and incapable.

I am always screwing up. No one likes me.

I disappoint everyone around me. I can't do anything right.

I'm never going to get this business going.

I doubt I can find one person who hasn't felt the wrath of the A.N.T.S. The difference is, I believe, how long you allow them to take up space. They can visit, but don't let them unpack.

Know where the RAID is. According to Dr. Amen, every time you have a negative thought, your brain releases chemicals that make your body feel awful. However, the opposite is also true.

With positive thoughts, chemicals are released that make your body feel relaxed. Dr. Amen's findings include examples of how our thought patterns can wreak havoc by predicting the worst. He shares that most panic attacks happen because of the misfortunes we predict will happen, but never do.[2] There's the blame thought pattern too, where we blame others for our problems and never hold ourselves accountable. Though we may think blaming others for our circumstances soothes us in the moment, problems that haunt us will remain. It just doesn't work.

When my late sister-in-law Kim decided she was going to open a boutique in the midst of her battle with cancer, I didn't understand. I knew that Kim was a smart woman and a great mother, but a business woman? She fell in love with my brother Jamie when she was only nineteen years old. On Christmas Eve, 2019, Kim, age forty-six at the time, sat my brother down to tell him that she was diagnosed with Stage 3 triple negative breast cancer. Her strength in this one act speaks volumes. My brother had no idea she was that sick, and that she was carrying the burden quietly while waiting for results.

For most of her life, Kim was a stay-at-home mom who concentrated on raising four healthy children. When she wasn't preparing countless meals, washing piles of clothes or reading to her children, she was advising and tracking business transactions that she and Jamie did together. Properties. Repairs. Bills. Later, she added her managerial job at a clothing store to her list of responsibilities. While battling cancer and the brutality of chemotherapy, Kim demonstrated what I'm sharing here. When we become consistent in the power of our thoughts, anything is possible. As a woman, a mom, and a patient, she wanted to leave a legacy to her children. So, she aptly named her boutique Wild Phoenix. You can visit Wild Phoenix on 8th street in Ocean City, New Jersey. You can't step inside her vision without getting a sense of Kim's style and personality. The store's design is chic, the atmosphere is friendly, and the clothes are comfortable, practical, and cute: Kim.

While she was dying, Kim wanted to emphasize living. She felt driven to teach the most valuable lessons she could to her children. Lessons of strength, hope, opportunity, and compassion. She was incredibly successful. When she lost her battle on July 6, 2022, more than four hundred people gathered on the beach to celebrate her life as she'd envisioned it. She wanted no tears. No pity. She wanted the simplicity of a life enjoyed and appreciated through good food, hugs, and shared memories. Her goal was that families would gather in her memory on a beautiful beach surrounded by love. She was so brave and so private about her battle that her loss was a shock to her community. No one had any idea how sick she was. While cancer would destroy her body, it was powerless against her positive mindset. Kim's journey reaffirms the theme of this chapter. The importance of our thoughts, words, and perspective play a much larger role in our mindsets than we're often willing to admit. They can be bigger than cancer. They can be bigger than fear. They can be bigger than pain.

In the decades I got to love Kim, she had that effect on me. She consistently demonstrated that power. Nothing and no one could take that away from her. Kim slept so soundly towards the end, but when my brother Jamie whispered, "I love you Kim" in her ear, she mouthed it back. Her body was completely failing her, but against all odds, her mind was powered by love. We can all learn from Kim's life. I hope she knows how her heroism brought out the best in us. Her example taught us more about acceptance, humility, and forgiveness. Her example has made us love more and complain less. Her example lives on in everything we do. I can't imagine what Kim was thinking as she started hospice. What I do know is that her battle was her least concern. She still cared for us. She still showed us love. She still wanted the best for her children and she still, somehow, made us laugh. Even in those last days it was not about her, only about the people she loved. You can't witness that love without it changing the way you love. I am guessing that someone in your life has shown up for you as Kim did for me. Let their example fill your heart and your progress.

As of this writing, it's been eight months since I have held Kim's hand and these words were accompanied by overwhelming grief. So I did something. I thought about how she planted the seeds for our lives without her in it. She kept notes about her journey. She wrote cards to her kids. She had visits with friends and family to share her love and her appreciation.

Decades ago, when Kevin was sick, he wanted a garden. It was the first time we ever planted peas. They were so amazing they never made it into our kitchen: We ate them straight from their soft vines. I put on sunglasses to hide my tears and drove to the nearest garden center. There I bought just one pack of seeds. I put them in the ground on March 17th, St. Patrick's Day. While I dug and patted and watered, I thought of Kim. I thought of the roses she planted out front of her house. I thought of the seeds she planted in the heart of every person who knew her.

Every action we take is planting a seed for growth.

When we speak with compassion, we are planting seeds of love. When we listen attentively, we are planting seeds of communication.

When we reach out to help, even when hurting, we are planting seeds of hope.

Questions to consider:

Do you have an A.N.T. problem? Are you ready to do some stomping?

What will you do the next time you use negative self talk?

Do you see the glass as half full? Or half empty? The proverbial phrase is worth considering. Do you celebrate how far you've come or do you fear how far you still need to go?

Are your thoughts goal or worry driven?

Noteworthy:

Grab a mason jar and title it: Positivity jar. Every time that you change your wording to reflect hope, write your words on a paper and add them to your jar. Fill your jar!

Acknowledging our perspectives is the first step in changing the conversation... even one with yourself.

---

1. Senanayake, Sanuja. "All That We Are Is the Result of What We Have Thought | Sanuja Senanayake." *Sanuja Senanayake*, 9 Jan. 2021,http://sanuja.com/blog/all-that-we-are-is-the-result-of-what-we-have-thought#:~:text=Over%20 2500%20years%20ago%2C%20a,applicable%20principle%20in%20modern%20societies.

2. *Negative Thoughts and Brain Health | Amen Clinics.* http://www.amenclinics.com/blog/do-you-have-an-ant-infestation-in-your-head. 0.

Chapter Nine

Good Will Hunting: Reframing Your Life After Loss

"To know even one life has breathed easier because you have lived. This is to have succeeded." -*Ralph Waldo Emerson*

Your heart knows what you want. As for myself, I knew I wanted to get married and have children. I knew that I wanted to spend my life working with kids. From the time I hit double digits, I was aware that too many children face hardships, neglect, hunger, and abuse. I recognized that while adults can make decisions to possibly change their outcomes, children must depend on capable adults to change theirs. It's not fair.

I gave birth to Alina Nicole O'Donnell on August 28, 1992 and named her after Alina Enggist. I was a nanny for the Enggist family throughout college and learned that the name Alina is of Slavic origin meaning "bright and beautiful."

Alina Enggist was given the perfect name. So was Alina O'Donnell, with her rosy cheeks, strawberry blond hair, and green eyes.

She was our world: precocious, funny, creative, and a sweet child who brought so much love and endless entertainment to our family.

Kevin was diagnosed with ALS while Alina was just a toddler, and my immediate sadness was reserved for her. He would not be able to play with her, dance with her, or walk her down the aisle. She would be accomplishing new skills as Kevin would become dependent for help with those same skills. Walking. Eating. Speaking. Bathing. I was going to lose my husband; and Alina her father. It would happen before she was old enough to remember his voice, his sense of humor, his favorite music, and the way he gave her Eskimo kisses.

In June of 2000, another family, not too far from us, was also facing ALS. Warren Benton and Tina Singer Ames had just been told that Tina had ALS. Tina fell to her knees and cried, "But who will raise my children?" Her question was selfless. Her concern was more about the wellness of her children than her own disease. When Benton shared Tina's words with me, my heart sank. I could not imagine leaving my daughter, I didn't want to imagine leaving my daughter and sadly, both Kevin and Tina had to leave us all.

I wish that I'd known Tina, but from what I'm told, we shared the same love and adoration for children. When Benton and I married years later, I became what I affectionately call a bonus mom to Nora and Adam. Some people say a step mom and that works too, but I prefer bonus mom because I get to love more children than I thought I'd ever have. To this day, I continue to include Tina in my thoughts and actions when I am nurturing her children. Alina, Nora, Adam, Tina, and Raquel have taught me so much about the role of motherhood and absolute love. Really, the best things life has to offer begin from a place of love. That's where Hope Loves Company started and when I founded it, I became a mother figure to even more children.

When I was a teacher, I used to say that teaching is the only job where you are a parent, nurse, writer, actor, artist, singer, advocate, and educator. When you create a mission that involves children, you feel responsible for all of the children you serve like they're your own. My role at Hope Loves Company wasn't very different. Today, as it has always been, I fall in love with every child I meet. Through HLC I know that like my children, they will lose someone they love to ALS. They will feel broken. Like them, there have been times when I felt broken too. Seeking wholeness is why we keep going.

My late husband Kevin's death in 2001 left me feeling hopeless, something I'd felt before. Consciously, I knew that I was fortunate. I had a beautiful daughter. A wonderful Family. Supportive Friends. My health. So much for which to be thankful. Subconsciously, I had no idea how to go on. I wasn't sure I wanted to. I'd been a caregiver for nearly six years. I left my job. I left my hobbies. I spent my days keeping my husband alive. I did his grooming and his haircuts. I did his range of motion. I read his lips so that he could communicate. I got him in and out of bed with a hoyer lift. I cleaned his trach. I gave him his tube feedings and cleaned his port. I massaged his atrophied muscles. I brushed his teeth. Gave his meds and feedings at night.

Showered him. Turned him side to side throughout the night. Helped him with the urinal. If I was lucky, I got to eat. I got a few hours of sleep. I got to snuggle with Alina. When my husband died, I no longer knew who I was.

Grief is a very powerful feeling. Back then, I knew very little about it. I knew that crying was a sign of grief. However, I did not know the terms anticipatory grief or complicated grief existed. I didn't know there are both emotional and physical manifestations of grief. I didn't know that my memory was affected by grief, my stomach issues, headaches, and more. Grief is a topic that we need to know more about but are apprehensive to address. No one wants to talk about grief until they are grieving. Emotions researcher Dr. Brene Brown has found that *"each person's grief is as unique as their fingerprint. But what everyone has in common is that no matter how they grieve, they share a need for their grief to be witnessed. That doesn't mean needing someone to try to lessen it or reframe it for them. The need is for someone to be fully present to the magnitude of their loss without trying to point out the silver lining.*"[1]

She also shares that when grief is a part of your story, it needs to be shared. It wasn't until I started to really express my journey with grief that my journey got lighter. With every speaking engagement, written blog, authored book, and support group discussion, I became lighter. Brene Brown continues to tackle strong emotions like grief. "*We run from grief because loss scares us, yet our hearts reach toward grief because the broken parts want to mend.*" My heart reached toward grief, I needed to talk about it. Every time I shared stories about Kevin, his disease, his courage, I was processing what happened to him. What happened to us.

I was so sad. I heard, "You are young, you'll remarry."

"Give it a little time, you'll be fine."

None of those comments were helpful. To this day, I never tell anyone who has been widowed that it will get better or easier. I let them tell me what they think and I share my experience. My favorite contribution to the subject is a video that best puts the feeling into words. "You don't move on from grief, you move forward with it,"[2] said writer, podcaster and speaker, Nora McInerny.

In McInerny's funny yet poignant TEDx talk, she brilliantly put into words the reality of grief. Everywhere I looked in my house, I saw Kevin. I saw him smile as he watched the Eagles win. I saw him smile as he watched Alina read to him. I saw him smile with his family and friends who made him laugh, shared a beer, and placed a bet on who'd get voted off the island in Survivor. I also saw him sad. When he lost his father, his trach silenced his verbal grief, but his tears never stopped. When he could no longer hold Alina in his arms. When I started to struggle reading his lips. As a couple, we never asked why. When Kevin died, I asked how. How do I explain to a nine-year-old child that her daddy is gone? How do I check the box that says widow from now on? How do I keep Kevin's voice alive? How do I go on without him? Caregiving changed me. Losing my husband changed me even more.

I wish I'd known my friend Christopher MacLellan back then, but I'm grateful I know him now. Chris was a caregiver and he too was widowed. He gets it, and that's why he founded the Whole Care Network, where my podcast is hosted. Chris lost his partner Richard to cancer and that experience launched his entire purpose. He not only started WCN, but he has written books and is writing a screenplay.

When I interviewed Chris for *Gratitude to Latitude*, he explained my needs as a caregiver perfectly. *"What's so important in this vast network of caregiving is to give back from your experience. I was blessed to have a wonderful caregiving experience, as the years have gone now, it's seven years since Richard made his life transition. You find your path and your way in your own time. For each person, the caregiving journey is different. Life after the caregiving journey is different as well. I created the Whole Care Network as a tool for caregivers to share three things: validation, resources, and respite. I believe that when these are shared from one caregiver to another, they're the most trusted resources that a caregiver can have. You know they've been in the trenches too."*

I'd been in the trenches. I wanted validation, resources, and respite. Chris created something meaningful out of his loss and I needed to do the same. Hope Loves Company was one way of emerging after losing Kevin- one very healing way. In memory of my husband, I created something beautiful. I got to utilize all my former self before the years of caregiving and forgetting who I was. I got to dream. I got to write. I got to plan. I got to think about something bigger than myself, my loss, and my pain. A dream of creating a nonprofit would never have happened without my friend Linda Cassidy. Linda welcomed late night calls, listened to a plethora of ideas, delved into 501 c3 research and gave me the courage to try.

Here's what you need to know about friends: Choose them wisely. There are friends who are acquaintances. There are friends who are like family. There are friends who you don't see for years, but when you reunite, you feel that time preserved your love and connection. Friends are your chosen family. Choose them with the utmost conscious care and nurture those relationships. When you're young, your friends are made by proximity. As you get older, your world opens and so does your ability to meet and grow your friendships. Sometimes you get really lucky, and those best friends are with you for a lifetime.

When Linda experienced hardships in her life, I was there. When I experienced hardships in my life, she was there. That will always be the case. When I decided to put my grief into change for good, she raised her hand to volunteer. I will never forget the day we shared at the Fairview Lakes YMCA, to host the first ever Camp HLC weekend–a retreat for children who love someone with ALS. When we took the tour, I had massive Deja-vu. The dining hall looked familiar. The cabins too. Then, it hit me. Fairview Lake YMCA is exactly where I'd spent a weekend learning how to be a student council leader. Thirty-five years later, everything had come full circle. Occasionally, we get a perfect moment, where we trust and feel that our lives are on a greater path. That was one for me.

Every May, nearly one hundred children and their parents, whose lives have been affected by ALS, arrive at Fairview Lake YMCA at no cost to them. They're there to have fun, share resources, learn coping skills, and enjoy nature, all because good people worked together to create something life-changing. Hope Loves Company (HLC) - the mission, the people, the programs, restored hope in my life.

Self-awareness has taught me that no one succeeds alone. That's why all of the Academy Award-winning speeches are accompanied by a list of people to thank. My husband, Benton, my children, my family and friends all asked how they could help when Hope Loves Company was just a dream. They began by believing in me. Then they helped with all matters that were foreign to me: creating a website, reading legal documents, writing a mission statement, hosting a fundraiser. I learned how ALS affected Benton, Nora, and Adam, and I knew that we were united in hope. My husband never once said, "No," to the growth of HLC. My dream would have been impossible without his constant cheering and willingness to partner in this entrepreneurial decision. He has traveled to camp, driven us around, hauled boxes, corralled sugar-high kids.

He's done it all for years, without fail and without applause.

If I didn't think of others and their needs, there would be no Hope Loves Company. If I didn't choose hope over pain, I might still be immobilized and in bed grieving. If I didn't choose love again, I wouldn't be the proud wife, mom, and grandmother I am today.

At the beginning of this book, I shared my love for children. HLC has widened my ability to love countless children exponentially. That love is always being reciprocated. They call me. They visit me. They write to me. Sometimes, they even take me to lunch! My work with children, whether with my own or my extended children, continues to make me a better person. The best things that have ever happened to me, outside of my family, have been the result of servitude. Volunteering is a powerful gift to everyone. While we volunteer to help others, we can't help but to help ourselves in the process. When you allow moments of joy to return in your life, so will hope.

Volunteering can help you to:

SHIFT YOUR PERSPECTIVE IN THE SPIRIT OF SERVICE.

LEARN ABOUT NEW CAREERS.

BUILD SELF-ESTEEM.

MEET NEW PEOPLE.

ACQUIRE NEW SKILLS.

GAIN EXPERIENCE.

If you haven't looked into volunteering, it's time to begin the process. You never know where that new adventure will lead.

Questions to consider:

Do you want to volunteer from home or in person?

Do you want to work independently or in a group of people? Do you want to work primarily with adults, children, animals? What social and cultural issues are important to you?

What skills do you bring to a nonprofit organization?

Are you looking for hands-on experiences or an administrative position of support like serving on a Board of Directors or a committee?

Noteworthy:

Check out these sites to learn more: Volunteermatch.org Dosomething.org Hopelovescompany.org

---

1. "Atlas of the Heart - Brené Brown." *Brené Brown*, 22 Feb. 2022, http://brenebrown.com/book/atlas-of-the-heart.

2. TRANSSION: LHX. "Unbreak My Heart | Podcast | Boomplay." *Boomplay Music - WebPlayer*, http://www.boomplay.com/podcasts/57953.

Chapter Ten

Anything and Everything: Behaviors, Habits, and Perseverance- Oh My!

"Every action you take is a vote for the person you wish to become."
-James Clear

In 2007, I came to a crossroad. I was raising teenagers, facing my grief, and trying to figure out my identity, much like my children. I knew I could continue wallowing in all that had happened, or I could be grateful for the life I was given and the possibilities to come.

I have witnessed many miracles in my lifetime. Some were spiritual in nature, and some have relied purely on grit. Witnessing something unattainable become reality before your incredulous eyes is like watching a magic show. *How is that even possible?*

Outside of my own life events, nothing has ever moved me quite like watching the father and son team, Dick and Rick Hoyt, in action. I really wanted to interview Dick and Rick on my podcast, but never got the chance. Nevertheless, I must include their effect on me and my healing. The summer I first saw them was unusually hot. We were all gathered at Mercer County Park in Ewing, NJ for the New Jersey State Triathlon. I was there supporting two family members competing, my sister-in-law Keiren and my late brother-in-law Jim. I parked close to the lake so I could cheer my family as they emerged from the lake swim. That's when I saw him: Dick Hoyt, well into his sixties at the time, emerging from the lake carrying his adult son Rick, who is completely paralyzed, in his arms.

The image was surreal. A lean and motionless man being carried in the arms of a much older, running man looked both awkward and impossible. Dick was doing what I thought was impossible. So it hit me once again: Perhaps many of the things I believe to be impossible are not? Not only was Dick Hoyt strong, he was beyond grateful for everything that had allowed them to compete. As Dick mentioned in an interview, "The best that has happened to me in my life has come from the worst that has happened to me in my life."

I learned three things at Mercer County Park that day. 1) Love is the most powerful emotion possible. 2) Anything is possible when love is the reason. 3) We are far more capable than our minds lead us to believe. Together, Dick and Rick Hoyt accomplished the unimaginable. Rick, who lives with cerebral palsy, was unable to communicate until the age of eleven when he was fitted with an electronic communication device. He later graduated from Boston University in 1993. With enormous grit, Dick carried his son through 72 marathons, 6 Iron Mans and over 3,700 miles across the United States. When we embrace the power of possibility and marry that with a giving heart, we are limitless. We can choose to find the courage to lead the way. I'm once again reminded that it's really never about the destination. The journey there holds the true value.

It's the journey that sculpts who we are and how we find our way. I guarantee that Dick Hoyt relied on daily habits and a routine that inspired his success. He is the billboard for Perseverance, literally: There's a billboard of Team Hoyt as part of the Inspiration, Pass It On campaign at the Philadelphia Airport. Coincidentally, Oprah's billboard is right next door. Our daily habits and our decisions to persevere allow us to embrace our potential. While I knew a lot about perseverance growing up, habits were a whole other topic. We didn't have the healthiest habits in our home. Sometimes, we don't know good habits until we step outside of our microcosm.

Every action we take is important to the person we become.

Every action brings us either closer or further away from our end goal.

My dear friend April, who I met in kindergarten and have only seen a few times since I was eight, taught me a valuable lesson about habits when I was a teenager. My childhood best friend and neighbor April moved away in elementary school. I was distraught. She moved a whopping three hours away to a town in Pennsylvania, and that might as well have been Japan to me–both culturally and geographically. For a while, April and her family took trips to visit family and us, but eventually, those trips were less frequent. By the time I was thirteen, I decided that I would visit April by myself. Linked by our rotary phones, April and I began to brainstorm. Soon her parents were helping and then, by some phenomenon, I convinced my parents to let me go by myself. I said goodbye to my family and hopped on a Greyhound bus. Once out of New Jersey and into Pennsylvania, hills appeared, and the bus grumbled through switchbacks. I arrived in Amish Country a tad nauseous and grateful to finally see my best friend again.

Things were very different in April's home, and I found it all very exciting, until I learned there was no television. How could anyone live without a television?

At our house, the news was on with the coffee pot in the morning and when dishes were being washed late at night. At April's, there were no *Jeffersons*, no *MASH*, no Archie Bunker. Her neighbors were corn crops and Mennonites. I remember wondering what kids did in the middle of nowhere. But April had lots to do. She rode her bike. She visited friends. She read. She sewed and drew and created. She also surprised me with a teddy bear that she made with her own hands and imagination. I looked in awe. The bear was cuddly and soft. It had plush brown fur, a round belly, and a perfect set of eyes and ears.

That's when it dawned on me: If I ever wanted to be creative, I needed time to learn and play. Suddenly, television was less enticing. From then on, if I watched television, I was also doing something else: folding laundry, exercising, sorting containers or socks. When I turned fifty-six, our lone television died. At first, it was an odd feeling to think that we wouldn't just replace it. What if we had company and they wanted to watch the game? No more New Year's Eve in Times Square? CBS Sunday Morning and a cup of coffee go so beautifully together. We never replaced it and instead, I started writing this book.

If it weren't for that long bus ride home from April's house, I probably wouldn't have adopted better habits. It was one of my first lessons as a young adult not found in a text book. It's a great big world, go explore it and the people in it too. My exposure to April's family opened my world. It started my love of travel. It started my interest in different cultures, beliefs and values. It started my love to try new things. Our personalities and progress rely heavily on the habits and company we keep.

Habits are the small decisions we make every day that create the life we practice. Sadly, one of the realities of life is that we'll eventually lose those closest to us. Those who have inspired our better habits and hope. I recommend you keep them close by remembering who they were and what they taught you.

One of those losses was my friend Sara, who lived next door to us and battled ALS. As I watched her get in and out of her car, I guessed that she had ALS before her doctor. A caregiver knows. When I think of Sara, I automatically smile. I teased her about being a princess, and she teased me about being a mess. My wardrobe and my personal style have always been safe, even dull. Tan, black, white. I bought my first pink heels under her tutelage. She introduced me to expensive lipstick, designer clothes, and incredible scents. At parties, she even donned a fascinator: Sara wore the small hat on her head, complete with mesh and feathers, as though a Royal, with complete confidence. With a smile and access to her personal collection, she persuaded me to do the same. She discouraged my inexpensive haircuts and suggested a real salon. Since her passing, I might fall short of her expectations, but occasionally, in her honor, I do something Sara-like.

Soon after Sara lost the ability to speak, and just a few months before she left us, with the help of an eye-controlled computer and my lip-reading skills, I interviewed her for my podcast. Sara was many things. She was beautiful, funny, smart, and creative. She was a leader. She was also fearless. She ran a marketing company, loved everyone, and was a celebrity in our hometown.

When I asked Sara for advice during our interview about success she said,

"Be the best you can on any given day. Be good to yourself, always nourish and help people. If one is fortunate enough to feel gratitude, I mean really goosebumps feel it, resilience follows. It's the feeling of pure joy in the most emotional way. The love that has been shown to me makes ALS a minor role. Don't get me wrong, ALS is cruel and sneaky. But when the day's over, I lie in bed, recounting my blessings, grateful, ready, and excited to encounter tomorrow."

Habits. When battling a terminal illness, Sara was the same person she was before her diagnosis. While her body failed her, she continued to consistently show up with dignity, integrity, and compassion. Her habits and perseverance were so ingrained in her mindset and behaviors that nothing–not the inability to walk, talk, or eat–changed who she was. With the help of others, she still always looked stunning. She still went to meetings and out to dinner frequently, she still hosted fabulous soirees, and she still decorated her house for every holiday. Sara taught me to take pride in who I am. She taught me to acknowledge my skills and talents.

She taught me to advocate for myself. I can still hear her words as I write this book. *"You need to write it. You need to share your shine with the world. Own it darling and keep looking forward."*

Every single one of us has something to offer the world. Across the board, we all want to feel loved, respected, fulfilled, and appreciated. The million-dollar question is, how? Every journey begins with understanding, knowledge, and application. It has taken me more than five decades to determine who I am and what I want with this one beautiful life. Today is a great day to begin your path to success. Find your fearless five, your resources, and your voice. Don't be dissuaded by A.N.T.S. - yours or anyone else's. Embrace your skills and seek answers in the areas you know little about. Reflect and change the habits and behaviors that no longer serve you. Then, give healthier ones your time and commitment. Try new things and meet new people. Be open to change and growth. That's what Raquel did. She owns her ticket to personal growth.

"I consider myself incredibly fortunate because I was always encouraged to pursue higher education. Despite my initial reluctance, I persisted in my studies and ultimately achieved a college degree. Although I struggled academically in high school and had reservations about attending college, my family's unwavering support and encouragement made all the difference in enabling me to achieve this milestone. Looking back, I'm grateful for the opportunity to have pursued my education and the valuable life lessons I gained along the way. Developing good habits has taught me the importance of practicing patience and self-compassion. Instead of getting down on myself for slipping back into old habits, I approach each situation with kindness and a willingness to make things right. For example, if I forget to make my bed in the morning, I commit to doing it before I go to bed. This mindset allows me to still make progress towards my goals, even if I'm

not perfect in every moment. The '1 percent rule' has been a valuable tool in my journey towards self-improvement. By aiming to do something just 1 percent better than the day before, I am able to maintain a positive and proactive mindset, even on days when I'm feeling less motivated. This approach has been instrumental in helping me to build positive habits and achieve my goals."

Questions to Consider:

What daily habits serve you well?
Which ones need your attention?
How do you keep track of your action steps?
Do you prefer a paper or digital planner to get you organized?

Noteworthy:

I love physical paper calendars. Here are two that I have used:

Big A## Calendar Club: https://jesseitzler.com/pages/big-a-calendar

Happy Planner: https://thehappyplanner.com/collections/happy-planners

Chapter Eleven

Hope Personified

"Keep some room in your heart for the unimaginable."
-Mary Oliver

When I think of my brother Jamie, I think of endless talent. I can't think of anything he can't do. Ok, he can't sing, but he tries and that counts. He is the only person I know who somehow fashioned a completely functional boat cover out of household scraps. "You sew too?" He can also buy an old house, have a vision immediately for its potential, then with his own hands, not only create the blueprint, but build the remodel himself. Walls. Floors. Stairs. You name it.

Really when I think of my brother, I think of Maria Forleo's book, *Everything is Figureoutable*. [1] He figures it all out. It's a family trait. No matter the challenge, we figure it out.

Jamie and I are twenty-two months apart. I was born on Christmas Day; he was born on Mischief Night.

But there is nothing mischievous about him.

While Kevin was facing ALS, my brother gave us many gifts. His time. His money. His skills. When Kevin became bed ridden and could no longer get outside easily, my brother built a large birdhouse that would have been the pride and joy of any little girl, because it was a dollhouse- for birds. It was a charming Victorian, with a cozy wraparound porch, many windows and an ornate red door that was adorned with a tiny set of lovebirds that my brother carved with even tinier tools. Within days, birds flocked to our backyard where Kevin could see them from his hospital bed.

As if that was not enough, my brother was a magician. With clever planning and meticulous timing, he figured a way to bring the beach to us. He personified hope in a moment.

I wrote about that moment in time years ago in a blog:

The year was 2000 and it was a few days after Labor Day. At six a.m. I quietly rolled out of the twin bed in which I slept. My bed was adjacent to Kevin's hospital bed. The hum of his ventilator could have easily rocked me back to sleep, but I had work to do. I shuffled out of my slippers and night clothes and into my day clothes and clogs. My husband Kevin was asleep and so was our daughter, Alina then eight-years-old. Alina would need to go to school in a couple of hours and I would need to help Kevin out of bed, and ready for a new day.

But at this very moment, I had some quiet time to myself. I walked into our kitchen where Kevin's nurse sat, drinking coffee. I gave her a hug and put on my light jacket. I drove two blocks to the nearest Wawa convenience store and got my regular fix, a hazelnut latte, bagel and newspaper. Then I sat in my car, with the radio humming softly and took sips of the hot, creamy caffeine. The bagel and paper remained untouched. It was too early to be hungry: was too early to read what was happening in the world. Instead, I cherished the coffee and enjoyed my solitude. For those ten minutes, my life was normal. I was a mother, a wife and a worker prepping for my day like everyone else. However, nothing about my life was normal.

That sacred space, where I could sit and sip and cry, was what I needed at the hour to prepare for the challenges the day would bring. Soon, I would be back at home, waking Alina and getting her breakfast. Then, I would gently wake my husband, who was, for the fifth year, bravely battling ALS or Lou Gehrig's Disease. Kevin was now paralyzed; he was unable to speak and he relied on a feeding tube for nourishment and a ventilator to breathe. The physical Kevin, the one who went skiing, who played touch football, who mowed the lawn and hugged me tight, no longer existed. Yet, he was my love, my hero and my world and I would gratefully spend the day taking care of him in every way possible. Before my coffee was gone, when there were no more tears streaming down my face, I gathered my strength and drove home. I looked at Kevin's nurse, "Is he still sleeping?"

"Like a baby," she whispered.

I headed upstairs to wake Alina, cared for her and we headed to the bus stop.

I encouraged cheerful talk on our walk, but inside my heart was aching. The calendar said September and that meant Fall, soon to follow, Winter and if getting out as a family was tough in September, it was nearly impossible in February. I may have been crying for many reasons on that walk, sheltered by my shades, but at that moment I was mourning our losses as a family, and the reality of becoming a widow.

While a day at the beach sounded blissful, it was too much to ask for Kevin. A day at the beach was like running a marathon, an extraordinary event. It would mean having help with us, having medical equipment, keeping the wheelchair and medical equipment free of water and sand, it would mean keeping Kevin cool and comfortable and days of exhaustion to follow.

As I crossed the street on my way home from the bus stop, I saw my brother's pick-up truck parked in our driveway.

"Wow, it's early, what's he doing here?" I thought.

I loved when my brother visited. He gave me big hugs; he offered support both physically and emotionally to both Kevin and me. He was a loving uncle to Alina and he was very generous with the little time he possessed.

My brother met me at the door.

"Don't come in yet," he said with a grin.

"Why?" I asked. "What's going on?"

"Everything's fine, just give me a sec," he assured me.

Moments later, Jamie joined me out front.

"Ok, just trust me," he said. Then he covered my eyes with a scarf and took my hand.

I would have then and still would trust him with my life, so holding his hand as I walked blindfolded into my home was easy. Once inside, he asked me to sit down.

He then took off my shoes and socks.

"Jamie, what are you doing?" I asked again.

"Don't worry," he said in his gentle voice. "You will soon find out."

With my hand in his, I felt the carpet under my toes.

I heard the dishwasher running.

I heard the humming of Kevin's ventilator.

I heard the door to our patio open and took a guided step. My foot did not land on a brick patio as expected, but rather, on something cool and scratchy. I soon realized that my toes were sinking into sand.

It was a beautiful morning and the sand felt welcoming under my feet. Still blindfolded, Jamie then guided me to sit down on a towel.

He snuggled behind me and held me in his arms.

Seagulls screeched in front of me.

Mists of water speckled my face.

He handed me a hot drink and a treat.

We sat there, not needing to say anything. He embraced me while I sipped my coffee and nibbled my biscotti.

I had never made it to the beach that summer, but my brother brought it to me. To this day, that gesture of love is unparalleled.

When Kevin woke, my brother gently removed my blindfold.

I could see where I really was. Our patio was covered in sand. A CD player sat on the brick wall, from it came sounds of the ocean. He had supported a garden hose on a bucket and the water was set to sporadically mist.

With my eyes open, the beach faded.

But that memory, that sincere gesture of love and hope, will never disappear. This memory is hope in action.

I will spend the rest of my life mastering how to bestow this magnitude of hope to others.

I have no idea if you read Hope Givers straight through or one chapter a night. Perhaps you skipped around, and that's fine too. Maybe you are like me and juggle two books at a time, depending on your mood, maybe one fiction and one non-fiction. None of that matters to me. Here's what does: I hope that at least one of the stories within these pages inspired your journey. I hope that one tool was added to your list of resources. I hope that you stepped out of your comfort zone and committed to a new goal. I hope that you learned a few ways to improve your focus, your mindset, your self-care, and your relationships. I hope that you feel more hopeful about the direction you are heading. I hope that when you close this book, you feel empowered, connected, and grateful. I hope that you want to share Hope Givers with someone you love.

When you feel like you need a reminder, open this book again. Revisit the questions proposed throughout its pages, the answers you've since grown out of. Take your time.

Remember the incredible stories and exceptional people discussed in this book are just that: Stories and people. We are the hope givers. Nothing separates you from them, unless you want it to. The grit, perseverance, gratitude, and hope are yours to choose. They are yours to give.

---

1. "Everything is Figureoutable" - Marie Forleo" *Marie Forleo, 10 Sept. 2019,* https://everythingisfigureoutable.com/eif-a

About the Author

Jodi O'Donnell-Ames is a grateful mother, grandmother and proud Army mom. She is a hope giver who founded Hope Loves Company, the only non-profit with the mission of providing both educational and emotional support to children and young adults who love someone with ALS. Jodi is a coach and speaker who has penned two other books, *Someone I Love Has ALS*, which has helped thousands of people living with ALS, and a children's book, *The Stars that Shine*. Jodi's life of purpose has been captured in her TEDx talk: Living a Life With Purpose and her work has been shared on CNN, Steve Adubato Show, PBS, the Today Show and more. She is the recipient of numerous awards and likes to share coffee, hope and hugs. To learn more about Jodi, visit her website at www.joaspeakson.com.